Pub Walks & Cycle Rides

Northwest England

North West England

Walks and cycles in this book take in Cheshire, The Wirral, Lancashire and West Yorkshire. If you are seeking rural tranquillity, you can cycle on waymarked trails in Lancashire's largest forest, Gisburn Forest, walk through Macclesfield Forest or follow a route through a country park such as the Haigh Country Park. There is also a walk through Beacon Fell Country Park, an area which falls within the Forest of Bowland Area of Outstanding Natural Beauty, which was one of the first designated country parks in Britain. If you are looking for an easy-to-navigate route with watery views, walk around Anglezarke Reservoir in Lancashire or cycle around its neighbour, Lower Rivington Reservoir. Alternatively, walk by the Rochdale Canal or cycle along the towpaths of the Leeds to Liverpool Canal or the Macclesfield Canal.

If keeping family members entertained is key, plenty of routes have an attraction to visit on or near the route. There's the Anderton boat lift or the Lovell radio

Contents

ROUTE	TITLE	WALK OR CYCLE	PAGE
1	Thurstaston Common	🚶🚶	16
2	Willaston to Parkgate	🚴	20
3	The brine fields of Knott End	🚶🚶	24
4	Chester to Connah's Quay	🚴	28
5	Glasson Dock to Lancaster	🚴	32
6	Around Silverdale	🚶🚶	36
7	The Douglas Valley	🚶🚶	40
8	Burwardsley and Bulkeley Hill	🚶🚶	44
9	A circuit outside Frodsham	🚶🚶	48
10	Through Delamere Forest	🚴	52
11	Around Willington, Utkinton and Kelsall	🚴	56
12	Woods and heaths of Little Budworth	🚶🚶	60
13	Goosnargh and Beacon Fell Country Park	🚴	64
14	Rocks and water at Anglezarke	🚶🚶	68
15	Cuerden Valley to Preston and back	🚴	72
16	Around Rivington and its reservoir	🚴	76
17	Haigh Country Park	🚴	80
18	Around Comberbach	🚴	84
19	Wrenbury to Marbury	🚴	88
20	Hurst Green and the Three Rivers	🚶🚶	92

Picture on page 4: The Forest of Bowland, designated an Area of Outstanding Natural Beauty

Contents

ROUTE	TITLE	WALK OR CYCLE	PAGE
21	Darwen Tower and moors	🚶🚶	96
22	Gisburn Forest	🚲	100
23	A circuit from Barley	🚶🚶	104
24	Tatton Park to Dunham Park	🚲	108
25	Around Alderley Edge	🚶🚶	112
26	Down and up again to Mow Cop	🚶🚶	116
27	Foulridge to Greenber Field	🚲	120
28	The Bridestone Rocks from Lydgate	🚶🚶	124
29	On the packhorse trail along Salter Rake	🚶🚶	128
30	Around Lyme Park	🚶🚶	132
31	Middlewood Way	🚲	136
32	Tegg's Nose meadows	🚶🚶	140
33	From Wildboarclough to Macclesfield Forest	🚶🚶	144
34	A loop from Hebden Bridge	🚶🚶	148
35	Haworth's Brontë Moors	🚶🚶	152
36	Oxenhope and the Worth Valley Railway	🚶🚶	156
37	Halifax and the Shibden Valley	🚶🚶	160
38	A circuit from Wilmington	🚶🚶	164
39	Shipley Glen's Tramway and Baildon Moor	🚶🚶	168
40	A circuit around Holmfirth	🚶🚶	172

Locator map

telescope at Jodrell Bank, both in Cheshire, or the option of a trip on Britain's last remaining complete branch line railway, the Keighley and Worth Valley Railway. National Trust properties to visit on or after your walk or cycle include grand Tatton Hall (and park) in Cheshire, and Little Moreton Hall at Scholar Green, which is an exceptionally well-preserved half-timbered house. The house that you see on the walk around Lyme Park may seem familiar as it was the setting for the BBC's popular adaptation of *Pride and Prejudice* in 1994. Continuing the literary theme, you can visit the area which inspired Tolkein's writing of *The Lord of the Rings* trilogy and spot some familiar place names. If you are a Brontë fan, then the Brontë's parsonage at Haworth in West Yorkshire is a must.

If an interesting pub is the focus of your day, then try The Dusty Miller in Wrenbury, which is in a beautiful, converted 16th-century mill, or The Hark to Bounty, which served as a courthouse and still retains features such as jury benches and a witness box.

Above: The mill town of Hebden Bridge
Left: Marsden in West Yorkshire

Using this book

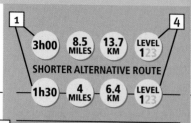

Each walk and cycle ride has a coloured panel giving essential information for the walker and cyclist, including the distance, terrain, nature of the paths, and where to park your car.

1 3h00 8.5 MILES 13.7 KM LEVEL 123

SHORTER ALTERNATIVE ROUTE

1h30 4 MILES 6.4 KM LEVEL 123 **4**

2 — **MAP:** OS Explorer OL24 White Peak

3 **START/FINISH:** Rudyard Old Station, grid ref SJ 955579

TRAILS/TRACKS: old railway trackbed

LANDSCAPE: wooded lake shore, peaceful pastures and meadows

PUBLIC TOILETS: Rudyard village

5 — **TOURIST INFORMATION:** Leek, tel 01538 483741

6 — **CYCLE HIRE:** none near by

THE PUB: The Abbey Inn, Leek, see Directions to the pub, page 27

7 — ❶ Take care along the banks of the lake – keep well away from the shore line

1 MINIMUM TIME: The time stated for completing each route is the estimated minimum time that a reasonably fit family group of walkers or cyclists would take to complete the circuit. This does not allow for rest or refreshment stops.

2 MAPS: Each route is shown on a detailed map. However, some detail is lost because of the restrictions imposed by scale, so for this reason, we recommend that you use the maps in conjunction with a more detailed Ordnance Survey map. The relevant Ordnance Survey Explorer map appropriate for each walk or cycle is listed.

3 START/FINISH: Here we indicate the start location and parking area. There is a six-figure grid reference prefixed by two letters showing which 100km square of the National Grid it refers to. You'll find more information on grid references on most Ordnance Survey maps.

4 LEVEL OF DIFFICULTY: The walks and cycle rides have been graded simply (1 to 3) to give an indication of their relative difficulty. Easier routes, such as those with little total ascent, on easy footpaths or level trails, or those covering shorter distances are graded 1. The hardest routes, either

because they include a lot of ascent, greater distances, or are in hilly, more demanding terrains, are graded 3.

5 TOURIST INFORMATION: The nearest tourist information office and contact number is given for further local information, in particular opening details for the attractions listed in the 'Where to go from here' section.

6 CYCLE HIRE: We list, within reason, the nearest cycle hire shop/centre.

7 ❶ Here we highlight any potential difficulties or dangers along the route. At a glance you will know if the walk is steep or crosses difficult terrain, or if a cycle route is hilly, encounters a main road, or whether a mountain bike is essential for the off-road trails. If a particular route is suitable for older, fitter children we say so here.

About the pub

Generally, all the pubs featured are on the walk or cycle route. Some are close to the start/finish point, others are at the midway point, and occasionally, the recommended pub is a short drive from the start/finish point. We have included a cross-section of pubs, from homely village locals and isolated rural gems to traditional inns and upmarket country pubs which specialise in food. What they all have in common is that they serve food and welcome children.

The description of the pub is intended to convey its history and character and in the 'food' section we list a selection of dishes, which indicate the style of food available. Under 'family facilities', we say if the pub offers a children's menu or smaller portions of adult dishes, and whether the pub has a family room, highchairs, baby-changing facilities, or toys. There is detail on the garden, terrace, and any play area.

DIRECTIONS: If the pub is very close to the start point we state see Getting to the Start. If the pub is on the route the relevant direction/map location number is given, in addition to general directions. In some cases the pub is a short drive away from the finish point, so we give detailed directions to the pub from the end of the route.

PARKING: The number of parking spaces is given. All but a few of the walks and rides start away from the pub. If the pub car park is the parking/start point, then we have been given permission by the landlord to print the fact. You should always let the landlord or a member of staff know that you are using the car park before setting off.

OPEN: If the pub is open all week we state 'daily' and if it's open throughout the day we say 'all day', otherwise we just give the days/sessions the pub is closed.

FOOD: If the pub serves food all week we state 'daily' and if food is served throughout the day we say 'all day', otherwise we just give the days/sessions when food is not served.

BREWERY/COMPANY: This is the name of the brewery to which the pub is tied or the pub company that owns it. 'Free house' means that the pub is independently owned and run.

REAL ALE: We list the regular real ales available on handpump. 'Guest beers' indicates that the pub rotates beers from a number of microbreweries.

DOGS: We say if dogs are allowed in pubs on walk routes and detail any restrictions.

ROOMS: We list the number of bedrooms and how many are en suite. For prices please call the pub.

Please note that pubs change hands frequently and new chefs are employed, so menu details and facilities may change at short notice. Not all the pubs featured in this guide are listed in the *AA Pub Guide*. For information on those that are, including AA-rated accommodation, and for a comprehensive selection of pubs across Britain, please refer to the *AA Pub Guide* or see the AA's website www.theAA.com

Alternative refreshment stops

At a glance you will see if there are other pubs or cafés along the route. If there are no other places on the route, we list the nearest village or town where you can find somewhere else to eat and drink.

☛ Where to go from here

Many of the routes are short and may only take a few hours. You may wish to explore the surrounding area after lunch or before tackling the route, so we have selected a few attractions with children in mind.

Walking and cycling in safety

WALKING

All the walks are suitable for families, but less experienced family groups, especially those with younger children, should try the shorter or easier walks first. Route finding is usually straightforward, but the maps are for guidance only and we recommend that you always take the suggested Ordnance Survey map with you.

Risks

Although each walk has been researched with a view to minimising any risks, no walk in the countryside can be considered to be completely free from risk. Walking in the outdoors will always require a degree of common sense and judgement to ensure that it is as safe as possible, especially for young children.

- Be particularly careful on cliff paths and in upland terrain, where the consequences of a slip can be serious.

- Remember to check tidal conditions before walking on the seashore.
- Some sections of route are by, or cross, busy roads. Remember traffic is a danger even on minor country lanes.
- Be careful around farmyard machinery and livestock.
- Be aware of the consequences of changes in the weather and check the forecast before you set out. Ensure the whole family is properly equipped, wearing warm clothing and a good pair of boots or sturdy walking shoes. Take waterproof clothing with you and carry spare clothing and a torch if you are walking in the winter months. Remember the weather can change quickly at any time of the year, and in moorland and heathland areas, mist and fog can make route finding much harder. In summer, take account of the heat and sun by wearing a hat and carrying enough water.

- On walks away from centres of population you should carry a whistle and survival bag. If you do have an accident requiring emergency services, make a note of your position as accurately as possible and dial 999.

CYCLING

Cycling is a fun activity which children love, and teaching your child to ride a bike, and going on family cycling trips, are rewarding experiences. Not only is cycling a great way to travel, but as a regular form of exercise it can make an invaluable contribution to a child's health and fitness, and increase their confidence and sense of independence.

The growth of motor traffic has made Britain's roads increasingly dangerous and unattractive to cyclists. Cycling with children is an added responsibility and, as with everything, there is a risk when taking them out for a day's cycling. However, in recent years many measures have been taken to address this, including the on-going development of the National Cycle Network (8,000 miles utilising quiet lanes and traffic-free paths) and local designated off-road routes for families, such as converted railway lines, canal towpaths and forest tracks.

In devising the cycle rides in this guide, every effort has been made to use these designated cycle paths, or to link

them with quiet country lanes and waymarked byways and bridleways. Unavoidably, in a few cases, some relatively busy B-roads have been used to link the quieter, more attractive routes.

Rules of the road

- Ride in single file on narrow and busy roads.
- Be alert, look and listen for traffic, especially on narrow lanes and blind bends and be extra careful when descending steep hills, as loose gravel can lead to an accident.
- In wet weather make sure you keep a good distance between you and other riders.
- Make sure you indicate your intentions clearly.
- Brush up on *The Highway Code* before venturing out on to the road.

Off-road safety code of conduct

- Only ride where you know it is legal to do so. It is forbidden to cycle on public footpaths, marked in yellow. The only 'rights of way' open to cyclists are bridleways (blue markers) and unsurfaced tracks, known as byways, which are open to all traffic and waymarked in red.
  - Canal towpaths: you need a permit to cycle on some stretches of towpath (www.waterscape.com). Remember that access paths can be steep and slippery and always get off and push your bike under low bridges and by locks.

13

- Always yield to walkers and horses, giving adequate warning of your approach.
- Don't expect to cycle at high speeds.
- Keep to the main trail to avoid any unnecessary erosion to the area beside the trail and to prevent skidding, especially if it is wet.
- Remember the Country Code.

Cycling with children

Children can use a child seat from the age of eight months, or from the time they can hold themselves upright. There are a number of child seats available which fit on the front or rear of a bike and towable two-seat trailers are worth investigating. 'Trailer bicycles', suitable for five- to ten-year-olds, can be attached to the rear of an adult's bike, so that the adult has control, allowing the child to pedal if he/she wishes. Family cycling can be made easier by using a tandem, as it can carry a child seat and tow trailers. 'Kiddy-cranks' for shorter legs can be fitted to the rear seat tube, enabling either parent to take their child out cycling. With older children it is better to purchase the right size bike rather than one that is too big, as an oversized bike will be difficult to control, and potentially dangerous.

Preparing your bicycle

A basic routine includes checking the wheels for broken spokes or excess play in the bearings, and checking the tyres for punctures, undue wear and the correct tyre pressures. Ensure that the brake blocks are firmly in place and not worn, and that cables are not frayed or too slack. Lubricate hubs, pedals, gear mechanisms and cables. Make sure you have a pump, a bell, a rear rack to carry panniers and, if cycling at night, a set of working lights.

Preparing yourself

Equipping the family with cycling clothing need not be an expensive exercise. Comfort is the key when considering what to wear. Essential items for well-being on a bike are padded cycling shorts, warm stretch leggings (avoid tight-fitting and seamed trousers like jeans or baggy tracksuit trousers that may become caught in the chain), stiff-soled training shoes, and a wind and waterproof jacket. Fingerless gloves will add to your comfort.

A cycling helmet provides essential protection if you fall off your bike, so they are particularly recommended for young children learning to cycle.

Wrap your child up with several layers in colder weather. Make sure you and those with you are easily visible by car drivers and other road users, by wearing light-coloured or luminous clothing in daylight and reflective strips or sashes in failing light and when it is dark.

What to take with you

Invest in a pair of medium-sized panniers (rucksacks are unwieldy and can affect balance) to carry the necessary gear for you and your family for the day. Take extra clothes with you, the amount depending on the season, and always pack a light wind/waterproof jacket. Carry a basic tool kit (tyre levers, adjustable spanner, a small screwdriver, puncture repair kit, a set of Allen keys) and practical spares, such as an inner tube, a universal brake/gear cable, and a selection of nuts and bolts. Also, always take a pump and a strong lock.

Cycling, especially in hilly terrain and off-road, saps energy, so take enough food and drink for your outing. Always carry plenty of water, especially in hot and humid weather conditions. Consume high-energy snacks like cereal bars, cake or fruits, eating little and often to combat feeling weak and tired. Remember that children get thirsty (and hungry) much more quickly than adults so always have food and diluted juices available for them.

And finally, the most important advice of all—enjoy yourselves!

USEFUL CYCLING WEBSITES

NATIONAL CYCLE NETWORK

A comprehensive network of safe and attractive cycle routes throughout the UK.

It is co-ordinated by the route construction charity Sustrans with the support of more than 450 local authorities and partners across Britain. For maps, leaflets and more information on the designated off-road cycle trails across the country contact

www.sustrans.org.uk
www.nationalcyclenetwork.org.uk

LONDON CYCLING CAMPAIGN

Pressure group that lobbies MPs, organises campaigns and petitions in order to improve cycling conditions in the capital. It provides maps, leaflets and information on cycle routes across London.

www.lcc.org.uk

BRITISH WATERWAYS

For information on towpath cycling, visit

www.waterscape.com

FORESTRY COMMISSION

For information on cycling in Forestry Commission woodland see

www.forestry.gov.uk/recreation

CYCLISTS TOURING CLUB

The largest cycling club in Britain, provides information on cycle touring, and legal and technical matters

www.ctc.org.uk

Thurstaston Common

WALK

Thurstaston

THE WIRRAL

Panoramic views from a
heathland crest, and the
edge of a grand estuary.

Thurstaston Common

This is a walk of two distinct halves. It's
unfortunate that the busy A540 underlines
this division, but there is much variety here.
You start near the shoreline but, saving that
for the end, climb long, straight Station
Road. This is an uninspiring opening but
easy and quick. The grand Church of St
Bartholomew signals the end of the
beginning and once the main road is
crossed you're on Thurstaston Common.

Many people expect a 'common' to be
open but the name really refers to common
grazing. Where this right is no longer
exercised, unless the land is managed
in some way, it's quite normal for it to
revert to woodland. In fact most of the
common is wooded but there are still good
open stretches of heathland.

Most of the ground is dry but there are
a few damp hollows. One is skirted early on;
in summer it's marked by the white tassels
of cotton grass. The wet patches are also
home to cross-leaved heath, not the ling and
bell heather of the drier areas – its flowers
grow in clusters rather than spikes. Also
found are sundews, low-growing plants with
reddish, hairy, sticky leaves. These trap
insects from which the plant absorbs
nutrients lacking in the poor soils.

Just below the summit you break out
on to a bare sandstone crest which gives
a view over the Dee Estuary and out to
sea. On a clear day the Great Orme behind
Llandudno stands out boldly. From the
summit the view spreads to include

Liverpool's cathedrals. The Forest of
Bowland and Winter Hill rise to their left,
and you can also identify Formby Point.

After retracing your steps as far as
the church, the second half of this walk
begins innocuously across farmland, but
as you descend towards the sea, there's a
moment of drama as you arrive at the ravine
of The Dungeon, complete with tiny
waterfall. Below this you join the old
railway, which is now the Wirral Way. Past
ponds, home to waterlilies and moorhens,
you soon reach the brink of the slope about
50ft (15m) above the estuary.

It's stretching it a bit to call it a cliff,
but it's steep enough to be no place to slip.
This is nearly the end of the walk, but you
may want to linger and savour the view
across the wide estuary to Wales.

the walk

1 From the car park, loop round past
the visitor centre and wildlife pond,
go out to **Station Road** and go straight up
for 0.5 mile (800m). At the top the route
swings right.

2 Turn left before the church and go up to
the A530. Go left, past the **Cottage Loaf**,
then go right through a kissing gate. Follow
the track straight ahead to the end of a
surfaced lane. Just before the lane, turn
sharply left onto a rising sandstone path
that leads up onto **Thurstaston Hill**, which
is a superb viewpoint. Return to the lane.

3 Go through the right-hand of two kissing
gates onto a broad path but soon go
right on a smaller path. Cross a track near
a cattle grid and take the left of two paths.

This swings left and crosses a clearing. On the other side, go right to meet a clearer path just inside the edge of the wood. Go left, following a fence line and, less obviously, the course of **Greasby Brook**.

4 Maintain roughly the same direction through the woodland until a boundary wall appears ahead. Turn left alongside it. Where it ends keep straight on, passing the model railway. Alongside **Royden Park** the wall resumes. Where it ends again turn left by a sign and map. Cross a clearing to a junction.

5 After 20yds (18m) you reach a kissing gate. Through the gate and keep on to pass **Benty's Farm**. About 100yds (91m) later, leave the broad track for a narrower path through bracken into woodland on the right. The path leads to a kissing gate at the end of the surfaced lane met on the outward route. Retrace your steps past the **Cottage Loaf** and down the top section of Station Road.

View from trees across Thurstaston Common

2h00 — 5.25 MILES — 8.4 KM — LEVEL 1 2 3

MAP: OS Explorer 266 Wirral & Chester

START/FINISH: Wirral Country Park at bottom of Station Road, Thurstaston; grid ref: SJ 238834

PATHS: some road walking, sandy tracks and bare rock, then field paths, 2 stiles

LANDSCAPE: woodland and heath, farmland, seashore

PUBLIC TOILETS: in Country Park visitor centre adjacent to car park

TOURIST INFORMATION: Birkenhead, tel 0151 647 6780

THE PUB: Cottage Loaf, Thurstaston

Getting to the start

Thurstaston is a straggling village along a busy road, 4 miles (6.4km) from West Kirby and 2.5 miles (4km) from Heswall. The start is at the bottom of Station Road, where there is a large car park adjoining the Wirral Country Park visitor centre.

Researched and written by:
Terry Marsh, Jon Sparks

Thurstaston

THE WIRRAL

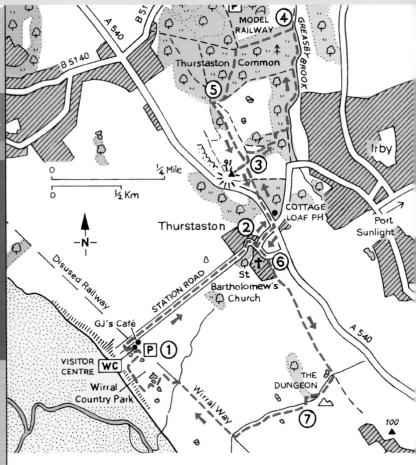

6 Turn left past the **church**. When the road swings round to the left, a lane continues straight ahead. Cross a stile and follow a well-marked footpath. In a dip, cross a stream and turn right at a footpath sign. After re-crossing the stream, zigzag down a steeper slope into **The Dungeon**.

7 Cross the stream again and follow it down. Climb on to an old railway embankment and go right. When green gates bar the way, sidestep left. Continue for another 220yds (201m) to a gap in the hedge. Follow a path, winding past a couple of **ponds** then out to the **cliff tops** above the

estuary. Go right for 240yds (219m), then bear right across grass towards the **visitor centre** and the car park.

what to look for

Thurstaston Common, despite its modest extent, is a real haven for wildlife. Listen for the curious laughing call of the green woodpecker, (probably the origin of its old name 'yaffle'), as well as the rapid drumming as it drills for invertebrates in tree bark. If you see one it will be unmistakable. Keep your eyes peeled and you might also see a fox – we did.

Cottage Loaf

Location, location, location... It's hard to resist the Cottage Loaf, which is passed twice during the walk, and is set in the beautiful surroundings of Thurstaston Common. Built during the 1920s in a traditional style, the interior is open-plan with comfortable seating and a pleasant dining area. There are warming and welcoming open fires for chilly winter days. There's plenty of outdoor seating too, and a delightful floral front terrace but children will need to be supervised as it all fronts on to the busy road and is unfenced.

Food

Expect an extensive menu listing light meals and main dishes such as fish pie, lasagne, salmon and spinach quiche, roast duck with orange and shallots, and chicken arabbiata.

Family facilities

Children are welcome in the pub until 8pm. Youngsters have their own menu and there are baby-changing facilities.

about the pub

Cottage Loaf
Thurstaston, Birkenhead
Wirral, Cheshire CH61 0HJ
Tel: 0151 648 2837

DIRECTIONS: beside the A540 in the village centre, at the junction with road to Irby (see Points 2 & 5)	
PARKING: 70	
OPEN: daily; all day	
FOOD: daily; all day	
BREWERY/COMPANY: Greene King	
REAL ALE: Greene King IPA, Cains Bitter	
DOGS: allowed in garden only	

Alternative refreshment stops

GJ's Café, by the car park entrance, is equally convenient and the standard café fare is well done and well priced.

☛ Where to go from here

Port Sunlight is named after a soap and built around a soap factory. The creation of William Hesketh Lever, later Lord Leverhulme, it's one of the country's finest garden villages, spread over 130 acres (53ha). At its centre stands the Lady Lever Art Gallery (www.nmgm.org.uk), noted for its collection of furniture as well as paintings and sculpture. Climb aboard the historic warships berthed in Birkenhead docks and view the finest collection of 20th-century fighting ships in the country – HMS *Portsmouth*, the submarine *Onyx* and a German U-boat (www.historicwarships.org).

Willaston to Parkgate

Start from an old railway station and follow the Wirral Way to a seafront resort with no sea.

Parkgate

Parkgate is unique in the North West; it looks very much like a traditional Victorian seaside resort with terraced houses, shops and hotels. Once the seafront gave onto golden sands, but the sea abandoned Parkgate more than 50 years ago, leaving the sands to revegetate into the grassy marshes you see today. The encroaching marsh finally reached the sea wall along The Parade at the end of World War Two. To the south of Parkgate, you can still find what remains of the Old Quay, evidence of the flourishing 16th century, now wholly landlocked. It is hard now to believe that once the water here was deep, and provided a safe anchorage.

Where the trackbed runs through the rock cutting, note the grooves made by the railway engineers as they cut through the sandstone bedrock. On one side, a lower wall and small sandstone cliffs are covered with mosses and ferns that love this kind of sheltered, moist environment.

the ride

1 Set off by riding to the far end of the car park and turning right through a narrow gap to gain the **Wirral Way cycle**

Shaded view across fields at Willaston

1h30 · **7.5 MILES** · **12 KM** · **LEVEL 1**23

MAP: OS Explorer 266 Wirral and Chester

START/FINISH: Hadlow Road railway station, Willaston; grid ref: SJ 332774

TRAILS/TRACKS: former railway trackbed, rough-surfaced and muddy in a few places, but generally in good condition. Short section of road, in Parkgate, which can be avoided by stopping before reaching it and returning from there

LANDSCAPE: mainly farmland, with light woodland along the old trackbed

PUBLIC TOILETS: at the start (in Ticket Office) and at Parkgate

TOURIST INFORMATION: Birkenhead, tel 0151 647 6780; www.visitwirral.com

CYCLE HIRE: none locally

THE PUB: The Nag's Head, Willaston

Getting to the start

The village of Willaston lies between Neston and Ellesmere Port, and is best reached from the A540, along the B5151, or from the M53 (Junction 6) along the B5133. The car park is at the former Hadlow railway station, just at the southern edge of the village.

Why do this cycle ride?

Tree-lined tracks, picturesque villages, an authentic railway station complete with ticket office, views of the Dee Estuary and the Welsh hills, rock cuttings and a wealth of wildlife – and delicious home-made ice cream available in Parkgate.

Researched and written by: Terry Marsh

track, which immediately passes the station platform, before reaching a gate. Cross the road with care, and continue on the other side, riding through lush arable farmland, along a fine corridor of trees and shrubs.

2 For a while after a **stone bridge**, the track is a little more rough, and runs on to a gate immediately before a road underpass. Go through the **underpass** and on the other side, pass through another gate to resume the Wirral Way. Eventually the track continues to run through a **railway cutting**, with steep sides and overhanging vegetation.

Railway station museum at Willaston, recalling early 20th-century rail travel

Optional Extension

Extend the ride a little by emerging with care onto the road, and riding to the right for just over 100 yards (90m), and, as the road bends to the right, leave it by branching left onto a continuation into **light woodland** of the Wirral Way.

Keep going as far as a bridge where the cycle route circles right and passes beneath the bridge, to go forward along an estate road leading down into Parkgate. At **The Parade** (the seafront), turn left. This is always busy, and it may be safer if parties with young children dismount and walk to the far end of **Parkgate**. Either way, press on to the southern end of Parkgate and turn left as the road now climbs steadily to return to Point 4 above. Turn right, back onto the original route and retrace the outward ride.

3 When the track emerges at a road (Mellock Lane) keep forward into **Station Road**, and cycle down to pass beneath a railway line and reach a small car park. Ride past this and resume the **Wirral Way**. Continue until the cycle route emerges near a car park, beyond which a broad track leads down to a main road on the edge of **Parkgate**.

4 Return from this point, back the way you came.

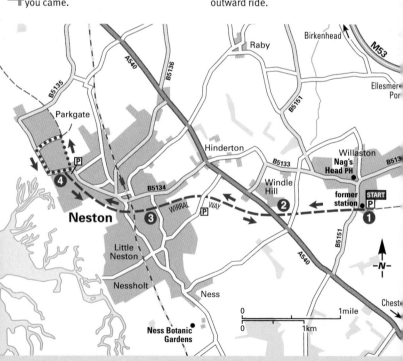

The Nag's Head

Built in 1733 and tucked away in the old part of Willaston, The Nag's Head is a welcoming pub to retreat to after the ride, with cushioned settles, comfy chairs and open log fires in the relaxing bars. In summer, the alfresco decking terrace with big benches and umbrellas provides a convivial setting for outdoor eating and drinking.

Food
Expect a straightforward pub menu offering snacks – ploughman's lunches and sandwiches – and main meals such as broccoli and cream-cheese bake, home-made steak and kidney pie, gammon steak and pineapple, and home-made curries.

Family facilities
There's a genuine welcome towards families and young children have their own menu.

Parkgate

CHESHIRE

Alternative refreshment stops
Pollards in Willaston and the Ship and the Red Lion on the Parade in Parkgate.

☛ Where to go from here
Discover how canals shaped Britain's heritage and see the world's largest collection of canal craft in a 200-year-old dock complex at the Boat Museum in Ellesmere Port (www.boatmuseum.org.uk). Ness Botanic Gardens overlooking the Dee estuary offer all round interest (www.nessgardens.org.uk), while the Blue Planet Aquarium near Ellesmere Port features two floors of interactive displays and an underwater moving walkway that takes you on a journey through the waters of the world. View huge sharks, deadly poisonous frogs and over 2,500 fish (www.blueplanetaquarium.com).

about the pub

The Nag's Head
Hooton Road, Willaston
Cheshire CH64 1SJ
Tel: 0151 327 2439

DIRECTIONS: in Willaston village centre on the B5133. Within walking distance of Hadlow Road Station

PARKING: 40

OPEN: daily; all day

FOOD: daily; all day until early evening

BREWERY/COMPANY: Enterprise Inns

REAL ALE: changing guest ales

The brine fields of Knott End

An easy walk exploring an unexpected and curiously salty corner of Lancashire's coastal plain.

Fields of brine

The salt industry here is not as ancient as that in Cheshire and has not had the same impact on the landscape, but it still had a significant role in the present scene.

Extensive deposits of rock salt lie below the surface around Knott End and Preesall and it is extracted by pumping fresh water down bore holes to dissolve the rock salt. The first such wells in this area were drilled in the 1890s and many of the well-heads remain.

Knott End today is a mixture of modest resort and commuter village. At low tide the sands are exposed for miles, far out into Morecambe Bay, and when it's clear the Lakeland skyline is a wonderful backdrop.

As you leave the built-up area, you meet the trackbed of the railway line that once linked Knott End to the main line at Garstang. The line was affectionately known as 'The Pilling Pig', a name derived from the note of the whistle of an early engine. The line closed in 1963. When you leave the old trackbed you climb a small rise – almost the only one you'll encounter on the whole walk – and from the far side, beyond New Heys Farm, you get your first sighting of the brine fields. To begin with they may look like nothing more than ordinary farmland, but then you will notice several pools – the walk soon passes close by one – left by subsidence.

As the walk continues, you'll see more reminders of the salt industry, especially

Walking the dog at the edge of a field, Knott End

along the track from the lane out to the sea wall. You follow this northward, with extensive creeks and salt marsh off to the left. Flying golf balls add spice to the next part of the walk. There's an interlude as you pass Hackensall Hall. The present building was erected in 1656 and was extensively renovated in the 19th century. There's more golf course to cross before returning to the sea wall for the last short stretch.

the walk

1 Go out to the **sea wall**, turn right past the ferry, along the road past the Bourne Arms and then along the **Esplanade**. Where the main road swings away, keep on along the seafront, down a private road then a short stretch of footpath. Where this ends, before a grassy stretch of seafront, go right down a short side street then straight across the main road into **Hackensall Road**. Go down this almost to its end.

2 Just before the last house on the left there's a **footpath** (sign high up on lamp-post) which wriggles round and then becomes a clear straight track. Follow this through a narrow belt of **woodland**, across open fields and then alongside a wooded

2h45 — **6** MILES — **9.7** KM — LEVEL **1** 23

MAP: OS Explorer 296 Lancaster, Morecambe & Fleetwood

START/FINISH: free car park by end of B5270 at Knott End; grid ref: SD 347485

PATHS: quiet streets and lanes, farm tracks and sea wall, 3 stiles

LANDSCAPE: short built-up section, seashore, farmland and golf course

PUBLIC TOILETS: at side of coastguard building adjacent to car park

TOURIST INFORMATION: Fleetwood, tel 01253 773953

THE PUB: Bourne Arms, Knott End

Getting to the start

Knott End lies at the northern tip of the River Wyre, just a short easterly ferry ride from Fleetwood. Getting there is a lovely convoluted drive across low-lying farmland from Poulton-le-Fylde or from the direction of Lancaster via Cockerham and Preesall. Free parking at the end of the Esplanade.

Researched and written by:
Terry Marsh, Jon Sparks

slope. Where the wood ends, go through an iron kissing gate on the right, then up the edge of the wood and over a stile into a **farmyard**. Go straight through this and down a stony track, which swings left between pools. It then becomes a surfaced lane past some **cottages**.

3 Join a wider road (**Back Lane**) and go right. It becomes narrow again. Follow this lane for about a mile (1.6km), over a slight rise and down again, to **Corcas Farm**.

4 Turn right on **Corcas Lane**, signed 'Private Road Bridle Path Only'. Follow the lane through the brine fields. After 0.5 mile (800m) it swings left by a **caravan site**.

5 Go right, past a **Wyre Way sign** and over a stile on to the embankment. Follow its winding course for about a mile (1.6km) to a stile with a signpost just beyond.

6 Go straight ahead on a **tractor track**, signed 'Public Footpath to Hackensall Hall 1m'. When it meets the **golf course**, the track first follows its left side then angles across – heed the danger signs! Follow the track to the right of **Hackensall Hall**. At a

Right: A rutted pathway at Knott End

T-junction go left on a track with a Wyre Way sign. This skirts round behind the **outlying buildings**.

7 The path swings to the right and then crosses the **golf course** again. Aim for a green shelter on the skyline then bear right along the edge of the course. Skirt round some **white cottages**, then go left to the sea wall. Turn right along it, and it's just a drive and a chip back to the car park.

what to look for

The well-heads, pools, and one small extraction plant all bear witness to the salt industry. The fields provide good grazing for dairy cattle and also for a large number of brown hares, which are larger than rabbits, with longer legs and ears. Hares don't burrow but rear their young in shallow scrapes in the ground.

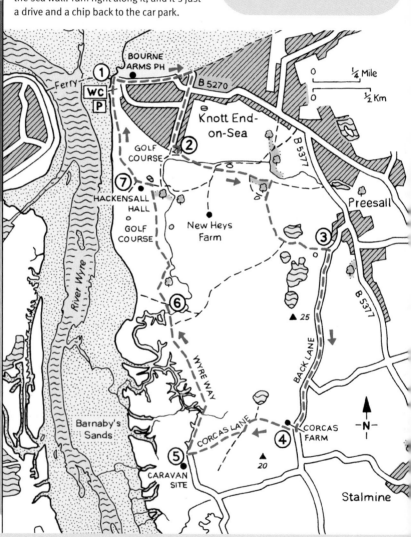

Bourne Arms

☞ Where to go from here
For most of the year, a small passenger ferry regularly makes the short crossing to Fleetwood. The town was planned as an integrated whole in the 1830s and 40s by the architect Decimus Burton, at the instigation of Sir Peter Hesketh-Fleetwood from nearby Rossall Estate. The Fleetwood Museum tells much more about the salt industry. Britain's oldest surviving tram system lInks Fleetwood with Blackpool.

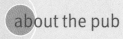

about the pub

Bourne Arms
Bourne May Road, Knott End
Lancashire FY6 0AB
Tel: 01253 810256

DIRECTIONS: see Getting to the start; pub is on the Esplanade (Point 1)	
PARKING: 20	
OPEN: daily; all day	
FOOD: daily; all day Sunday; no food Monday & Tuesday evening	
BREWERY/COMPANY: Free House	
REAL ALE: Flowers Original, Boddingtons, Greene King Abbot Ale, Timothy Taylor Landlord	
DOGS: allowed in tap room	
ROOMS: 3 en suite	

Close to the start of the walk and smack on the Esplanade with views across Morecambe Bay, the Bourne Arms is a large and rambling pub with cosy nooks and crannies inside and an airy conservatory dining room. Like the big, south-facing terrace, it makes the most of the wide sea views.

Food
Expect a wide range of traditional Lancashire dishes plus gammon, egg and chips, Cumberland sausage, lamb cutlets, grilled halibut, and salmon with horseradish sauce. There's also a choice of sandwiches and Sunday roast lunches.

Family facilities
Families are welcome in the eating areas of the bar and in the conservatory. Bargain children's menu.

Alternative refreshment stops
There's a café adjacent to the car park and a couple of others in the village.

Chester to Connah's Quay

Make the most of an enjoyable and easy ride along an old railway trackbed.

Trees on the trail

Along the old track are many plant species of the hardy type capable of thriving in the harsh conditions alongside railways. On this ride, keep an eye open for two types of tree: the elder and the willow. The elder produces lovely white flowers in summertime, and then supports huge clusters of lush black berries, which, although insipid when raw, produce a distinctly flavoured wine. The tree is also believed to hold mystical powers and many ancient superstitions are associated with it. In some English counties, it is considered unwise to cut the wood of elder without first securing permission by bowing three times before it, or by making an apology. It is also claimed that elder is a safe shelter in a storm, because the cross on which Jesus was crucified was made of elder, and so lightning never strikes it.

Willow is another tree that grows alongside this route, and it grows well on fertile riverside land. Cricket bats are traditionally made from willow, but it is thought unlucky to burn the wood, and few fenmen in the east of England will take willow into the house to burn, while there is a tradition in Lancashire that willow should not be burned on Bonfire Night. Have a look for the graceful weeping willow, which is found along the route; it is a tree that originated in China.

the ride

1 Leave the Northgate Car Park, and turn right along **Northgate Avenue**, soon

The cycle way on Hawarden Bridge across the River Dee

2h30 — **16.25 MILES** — **26 KM** — **LEVEL 123**

MAP: OS Explorer 266 Wirral and Chester

START/FINISH: Northgate Car Park (pay), Northgate Avenue, at the rear of the Northgate Arena; grid ref: SJ 406672

TRAILS/TRACKS: easy, surfaced track all the way, with two bridge crossings; a few barriers to contend with

LANDSCAPE: mainly farmland, but with some industrial sites

PUBLIC TOILETS: none on route

TOURIST INFORMATION: Chester, tel 01244 402111

CYCLE HIRE: Eureka Cyclists Cycle Hire, Woodbank, Chester, tel 0151 339 5629; www.eurekacyclists.co.uk

THE PUB: Northgate Arms, Chester

Getting to the start

The Northgate Car Park, is located at the rear of the Northgate Arena, a prominent building near the centre of Chester. Access is from a dual carriageway, the A5268 (eastbound).

Why do this cycle ride?

Although linear, the route is delightful in either direction. It offers very easy riding from the heart of Chester, out along a smooth-surfaced track all the way to the wharf at Connah's Quay. The route is being developed as a linear park and woodland, and crosses attractive countryside. Crossing the Dee at Hawarden Bridge is a highlight, with the end of the outward section then only a few minutes away.

Researched and written by: Terry Marsh

riding through a modern housing estate. At the far end of Northgate Avenue, go through a barrier into a small **park**, riding left on a surfaced track to emerge on the **former railway trackbed**, now surfaced. Turn left.

2 You soon cross the **Shropshire Union Canal**, and gradually the houses of Chester fall away, and the route enters a long stretch flanked by light **woodland**. Eventually, it passes into **Wales**, and open countryside with far-reaching views.

3 The A55 at **Sealand** is crossed by a new bridge, beyond which the route gradually starts to bend towards the River Dee and **Hawarden Bridge**.

4 Ramps lead up to a **cycle way** alongside the railway, and down the other side. Loop back left (animal grid to cross), and pass under the **bridge**, then continue once more on a broad surfaced track, which gradually veers right (after a barrier, and another grid) towards the long wharf and car park at **Connah's Quay**.

5 The return route is simply back the way you came.

Uninterrupted riding along a cycle way near Chester

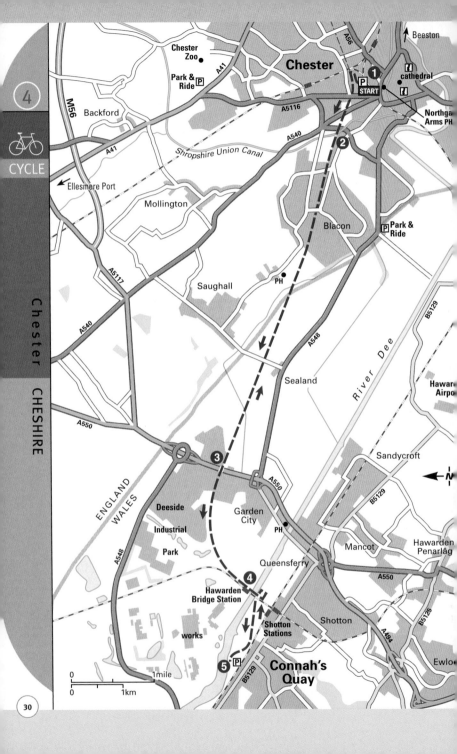

Northgate Arms

about the pub

Northgate Arms
Delamere Street, Chester
Cheshire CH2 2AY
Tel: 01244 372074

DIRECTIONS: beside the A5268 near the start of the ride. Best reached on foot from the Northgate Car Park, via subways beneath the dual carriageway

PARKING: limited (use Northgate Car Park)

OPEN: all day; closed Monday

FOOD: all day

BREWERY/COMPANY: Punch Taverns

REAL ALE: Courage Directors, guest beer

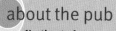

Despite its busy position beside the main dual carriageway through the city, the Northgate is relaxing and quiet inside, offering a haven away from the traffic, with soft sofas to sink into and warming log fires to warm your toes. Sporting memorabilia adorns the interior, including a pool table, which is fixed upside down to the ceiling – it's time to worry when you think you can pot any of the balls on it!

Food

The menu lists a wide range of pub food, from Cajun chicken salad, vegetable bake and scampi and chips to steak pie, lasagne, chilli, and locally made sausages with mash. Snacks take in sandwiches, baguettes and filled jacket potatoes.

Family facilities

Children are welcome inside the pub. There's a children's menu for youngsters and smaller portions are available. Small beer garden for summer drinking.

Alternative refreshment stops

If exploring Chester you'll find plenty of good pubs and cafés – seek out the Albion on Park Street.

☛ Where to go from here

Take a trip to Chester Zoo (www.chesterzoo.org), famous for its large enclosures and attractively landscaped gardens. With over 7,000 animals and 500 species there's much to see, notably the Tsavo Black Rhino Experience, the Spirit of the Jaguar and the children's Fun Ark Adventure playground. At the Blue Planet Aquarium (www.blueplanetaquarium.com), near Ellesmere Port, you can take a voyage of discovery along a 230ft (70m) underwater tunnel through the waters of the world and see giant rays and menacing sharks.

Glasson Dock to Lancaster

Follow the River Lune to explore Lancaster, and share the delights of its canal towpath on the way back.

Wildlife along the way

Aldcliffe Marsh is a Site of Special Scientific Interest because of its importance for waders such as redshank and lapwing. At one time the lapwing was a common sight on ploughed fields, but the use of insecticides and farming machinery has driven it to meadows and marshes in summer. Keep an eye open for the bright yellow ragwort, a plant that attracts the cinnabar moth, which lays its eggs on the stems and produces gaudy black-and-yellow caterpillars. In Freeman's Wood is a black poplar (*Populus nigra*), a native tree of lowland marshes and of this area, but not all that common. There are thought to be fewer than 3,000 black poplars in Britain today. The tree in Freeman's Wood is one of only two in Lancashire.

the ride

1 Begin from the large car park near the dock by crossing the road onto a cycleway along the edge of the **Lune Estuary**. A gravel track leads on to cross the River Conder before turning north through the **Conder Green car park**. (Follow the road right for The Stork pub.) Beyond the car park, ride onto a tree-lined track, and keep following this until it reaches a surfaced lane end, not far from the village of Aldcliffe.

2 Turn left into a **gravel area**, and then immediately, just before a footpath

stile, onto a broad vehicle track. At a cross-track, keep forward along a bridleway for **New Quay Road**, and going into **Freeman's Wood**. The track, now surfaced, crosses a section of **Aldcliffe Marsh**, and eventually comes out to meet a much wider road near a small light industrial complex. Keep forward until you reach an old arched bridge with the modern, **Millennium** (foot) **Bridge** near by.

3 Turn onto the footbridge, and then immediately right to leave it, without crossing the river. Go left on a surfaced **cycle lane** (signed for Halton and Caton). Follow the lane until it rises, to run briefly alongside the main road. Almost immediately turn right to perform a loop to the left into an **underpass** – you may need to dismount here. On the other side, go forward on a **signed cycle route**, which passes beneath a bridge and goes forward on a surfaced track down an avenue of trees. When it forks, keep left, and carry on to reach the stone **Lune Aqueduct**. Just before it, turn right onto a narrow path that leads to the foot of a flight of steps. Here you will need to dismount and carry your cycle up the steps to reach the tow path – a breathless few minutes, but well worth the effort.

Looking across the Lune to Lancaster

4 Turn right along the tow path. At **Whitecross**, dismount again to change to the other side of the canal. At a couple of places now you may need to dismount again as you pass canalside pubs, but eventually a **bridge** leads back over the canal. Over the bridge, turn immediately right down steps (dismount again) to rejoin the **tow path**.

5 Continue until you pass **Bridge 95**, following which the canal has a road on the right, and bends to the left. A short way on, leave the tow path and go onto the road (near a **lodge** on the right, dated 1827). Go forward, climbing steadily into the village of **Aldcliffe**. At the top of the climb, on a bend, take care, and turn right into the first lane on the right, descending quite steeply, and continuing down past **houses**, to ride along a narrow country lane to rejoin the outward near the gravel area.

6 Turn left onto the **trackbed**, and follow this back to Conder Green, turning left into the village for **The Stork**, or continue round the coast to **Glasson Dock**.

2h30 — **14 MILES** **22 KM** — **LEVEL 1** 2 3

MAP: OS Explorer 296 Lancaster, Morecambe and Fleetwood

START/FINISH: Quayside, Glasson Dock; grid ref: SD 446561

TRAILS/TRACKS: good route, though cyclists will need to dismount at a few points on the canal while passing waterfront pubs

LANDSCAPE: mainly old railway trackbed or canal towpaths

PUBLIC TOILETS: at the start

TOURIST INFORMATION: Lancaster, tel 01524 32878

CYCLE HIRE: none locally

THE PUB: The Stork, Conder Green

❗ Cycles will need to be carried up and down steps to reach the canal tow path

Getting to the start

Glasson Dock is on the Lune Estuary, 4 miles (6.4km) south west of Lancaster. It is best reached from Lancaster, or Cockerham to the south, along the A588, but may also be reached from Junction 33 on the M6 via Galgate – turn left at the traffic lights in the village centre and follow signs.

Why do this cycle ride?

A superb introduction to coastal Lancashire. The old trackbed and the return along the Lancaster Canal makes for easy riding, while the traffic-free cycle route through riverside Lancaster is ingenious. You can opt out at the Millennium Bridge and explore Lancashire's ancient capital.

Researched and written by: Terry Marsh

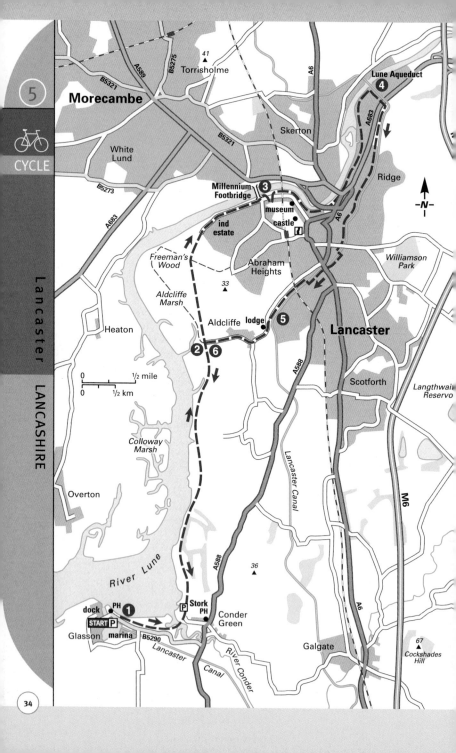

Morecambe

Torrisholme
41

White
Lund

B5321

B5275

B5321

A589

A6

Skerton

Lune Aqueduct
4

A683

Ridge

B5273

A683

Millennium
Footbridge
3

museum
castle
ind
estate

Freeman's
Wood

Aldcliffe
Marsh

Abraham
Heights

33

Williamson
Park

Heaton

Aldcliffe lodge
2 6 5

Lancaster

Scotforth

Langthwai
Reservo

A588

0   ½ mile
0   ½ km

Colloway
Marsh

Lancaster Canal

M6

Overton

River Lune

A588

36

A6

dock PH
START P 1

Glasson marina B5290

Stork
P PH

Conder
Green

Lancaster Canal

River Conder

Galgate

67
Cockshades
Hill

-N-

The Stork

about the pub

The Stork
Conder Green, Lancaster
Lancashire LA2 0AN
Tel: 01524 751234

DIRECTIONS: just off the A558 (west), a mile (1.6km) from Glasson and the start of the ride

PARKING: 40

OPEN: daily; all day

FOOD: daily; all day Saturday & Sunday

BREWERY/COMPANY: Free House

REAL ALE: Theakston Best, Black Sheep Best, Timothy Taylor Landlord, Marston's Pedigree, guest beers

ROOMS: 10 en suite

A white-painted coaching inn spread along the banks of the estuary, where the River Conder joins the Lune estuary and just a short stroll along the Lancashire Coastal Way from the quaint seaport of Glasson Dock. The inn has a colourful 300-year history that includes several name changes. It's a friendly, bustling and ever-popular place, the draw being the location, the range of real ales, and the rambling, dark-panelled rooms, each with warming open fires. The south-facing terrace and patio look across the marshes.

Food
Seasonal specialities join home-cooked food such as steak pie, locally smoked haddock, salmon fillet with bonne femme sauce, Cumberland sausage with onion gravy and mash.

Family facilities
Children of all ages are welcome and well catered for. There are family dining areas, family en suite accommodation, a children's menu, and a play area outside.

Alternative refreshment stops
There are plenty of cafés, restaurants and pubs in Lancaster.

☞ Where to go from here
A trip to Lancaster will be rewarded with a visit to the Maritime Museum, where the histories of the 18th-century transatlantic maritime trade of Lancaster, the Lancaster Canal and the fishing industry of Morecambe Bay are well illustrated (www.lancsmuseums.gov.uk). Take time to view Morecambe Bay or visit the Edwardian Butterfly House in Williamson Park (www.williamsonpark.com), or take a look at Lancaster Castle which dominates Castle Hill, above the River Lune. The Shire Hall contains a splendid display of heraldry (www.lancastercastle.com).

Around Silverdale

An easy-going walk, yet fascinating with its continuous changes of scenery.

A mosaic of habitats

The Arnside-Silverdale Area of Outstanding Natural Beauty (AONB) is intricate and exquisite. This walk tries the impossible, to sample all of its delights in one go.

The AONB covers a mere 29sq miles (75sq km) yet includes rocky coastline, salt marsh, wetland, pasture, woodland, heathland, crags and quarries, and some attractive villages, principally Silverdale in Lancashire and Arnside in Cumbria. With such a mosaic of habitats, it's no surprise that the area is rich in wildlife – more than half of all British flowering plant species are found here. There's a fine start, through Eaves Wood, then the route sidles through the back lanes of Silverdale before reaching the coast. The channels of Morecambe Bay shift over time and so does the shoreline. Changes to the course of the river now makes it impossible to follow the shore, at least at high tide. (Fortunately the footpath across The Lots, just above, offers a ready-made alternative.)

The route here avoids a tricky section of the coast south of Silverdale, returning to the shore near Jenny Brown's Point. After Heald Brow comes Woodwell, the first of three 'wells' (actually springs) on the walk. At Woodwell the water issues from the crag above the square pool. This was used for watering cattle but now you're more likely to see dragonflies. Woodwell and the other 'wells' around Silverdale occur where the water-permeable limestone is interrupted

by a band of impermeable material, such as clay. Rainfall generally sinks quickly into limestone and there are no surface streams over most of the area, so the springs were of vital importance. This rapid drainage also means that few of the footpaths are persistently muddy, even after heavy rain. Lambert's Meadow, however, is damp. It sits in a hollow where fine wind-blown silt (loess) accumulated after the last Ice Age. The soil is dark and acidic, very different from that formed on the limestone, and the plant community is different too.

the walk

1 From the end of the National Trust car park at **Eaves Wood**, follow the footpath to a T-junction. Go right a few paces then left between **old gate pillars**, climbing gently. At a fork, keep left to a ring of beech trees, then straight on. At the next junction, go forward, then bear left, down to a high wall and continue on this line to a lane.

2 Cross on to a track signed **'Cove Road'**. Keep ahead down a narrow path, a drive, another track and another narrow path to a wider road. After 200yds (183m) go left down a road leading to The Cove.

3 At **The Cove**, go left to white gate, and onto path for **The Lots**, climbing above cliffs to a gate. Cross a field (**Bank House Farm**) on grassy path to a gate in a wall. Then cross another field to **Stankelt Road**. Turn right to reach **The Silverdale Hotel**, just a short way further on round the corner.

Jenny Brown's Point is near the walk route

4 Return to the corner and go into Lindeth Road. Follow this as far as the turning at **Gibraltar Farm**. Go along this lane for 350yds (320m). Enter the National Trust property of **Jack Scout**.

5 Descend left to a **lime kiln** then follow a narrowing path bearing right. This swings left and later passes above a steep drop. Follow a clear path to a gate. After 100yds (91m), another gate leads into the lane. At its end bear right to pass below **Brown's Houses**. Follow the edge of the salt marsh to a stile, go forward to a **signpost**.

6 Turn left, climbing steeply to a gate at **Heald Brow**. Climb over rock and through a lightly wooded area into the open. Go left to cross a stile then alongside a wall to a **small wood**. From a gate, follow a walled path down right. Cross the road to a

| 2h30 | 5.5 MILES | 8.8 KM | LEVEL 2 3 |

MAP: OS Explorer OL7 The English Lakes (SE)

START/FINISH: small National Trust car park for Eaves Wood; grid ref: SD 471759

PATHS: little bit of everything, 6 stiles

LANDSCAPE: pot-pourri of woodland, pasture, village lanes and shoreline

PUBLIC TOILETS: in Silverdale village

TOURIST INFORMATION: Lancaster, tel 01524 32878

THE PUB: The Silverdale Hotel, Silverdale

Getting to the start

Silverdale clings to the northern edge of Lancashire, a few miles north of Carnforth off the A6 and the M6 (junction 35), and looks across the great expanse of Morecambe Bay to the Furness peninsula.

Researched and written by: Terry Marsh, Jon Sparks

Silverdale LANCASHIRE

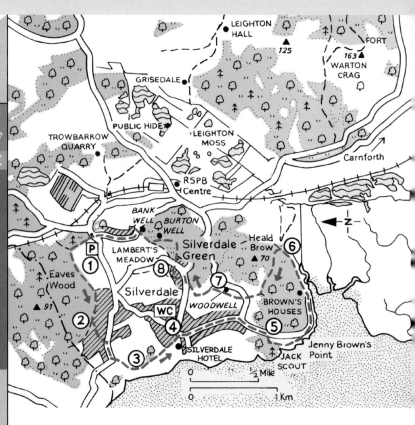

squeeze stile in a wall, descend, then walk below the crags to **Woodwell**.

7 The path signed '**The Green via cliff path**' leads to a rocky staircase. At the top go straight ahead to join a broader path. Follow it left to a gate, slant right, then continue left into woodland. Follow a **woodland path** to a stile on the right and a narrow section leads to a road. Go right 100yds (91m), then left into **The Green**. Keep right at a junction, then join a wider road.

8 Go left for 75yds (69m) then right, signposted 'Burton Well Lambert's Meadow'. The track soon descends then swings left, passing **Burton Well** on the right. Go through a gate into **Lambert's Meadow**, then go right, over a footbridge

to a gate. Climb up, with some steps, and continue more easily to a fork. Go left alongside a pool (**Bank Well**) into a lane. Go left and at the end the car park is virtually opposite.

The Silverdale Hotel

A listed coaching inn, built in 1836, and run by the Carney family since 1987, the Silverdale Hotel is a very popular pub with a warm and welcoming interior decorated with paintings of local and country scenes, ornaments and bric-a-brac, and a small conservatory where food is served overlooking the garden. The pub stands just a few minutes' stroll from the shore and has far-reaching views across Morecambe Bay. This is the ideal retreat for walkers on wild winter days.

Food
Wide-ranging menus offer a traditional choice of meals, including hot steak and onion sandwiches, filled jacket potatoes and salads, Cumberland sausage and mash, steak, ale and mushroom pies and a roast of the day. Puddings include sticky toffee pudding and speciality ice creams.

Family facilities
Children are welcome and the pub offers a children's menu as well as two family bedrooms.

Alternative refreshment stops
The tea room at Wolf House Gallery is a great spot for mid-walk refreshments, as long as you can find a table. For post-walk celebrations, you could also head for the New Inn in the nearby village of Yealand Conyers. There's good food and beer, a small cosy bar, a non-smoking dining room and a walled beer garden that's delightful on summer evenings.

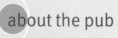

about the pub

The Silverdale Hotel
Shore Road, Silverdale
Carnforth, Lancashire LA5 0TP
Tel: 01524 701206

DIRECTIONS: village centre, along Shore Road; see Point 3	
PARKING: 30	
OPEN: daily; all day	
FOOD: daily	
BREWERY/COMPANY: Free House	
REAL ALE: Bass, guest beers	
DOGS: allowed in the bars	
ROOMS: 7 en suite	

☛ Where to go from here
The Leighton Moss RSPB reserve (www.rspb.org.uk) and nearby Leighton Hall (www.leightonhall.co.uk) are obvious attractions, but for something different (and free) pop in to Trowbarrow Quarry. Last worked in 1959, the quarry is now a Local Nature Reserve, and it's also a Site of Special Scientific Interest (SSSI) for its geology. Most striking is the near-vertical Main Wall, basically an upturned slice of fossil seabed.

Douglas Valley delights

Douglas Valley

LANCASHIRE

A gentle yet surprising corner of Lancashire, and it saves the best until last

Moor and valley

West Lancashire is full of surprises. The walk starts with a slight ascent on to High Moor. The 'high' part creeps up on you, unsuspected until you start down an enclosed track and then out into a field. The spire of Parbold church is below and, to its right, the land falls away to the lowlands around Ormskirk and away to the sea. Inland you look across the Douglas Valley to the ridge of Ashurst's Beacon, which is another grand viewpoint.

Now you amble down into the valley. Once this was a major communications corridor. First the river itself was improved for navigation in 1742, then came the Leeds and Liverpool Canal – the longest single canal in Britain. It carried stone from local quarries and coal.

The canal declined and fell into dereliction but the growth of leisure boating has brought a revival. Having climbed up a little from the canal, and crossed a few fields, you come to the Fairy Glen. Its origins are largely natural, rather than supernatural, and there are some traces of small-scale quarrying, but there is a kind of magic about the place. Dappled sunlight gilds the rocks and waterfalls. The ground under the trees may show wood anemones and celandines, wood sorrel, or carpets of bluebells and wild garlic. Between June and September, especially in the lower reaches, there are great drifts of white flowers on loose spikes. This plant is appropriately named for Fairy Glen: it is enchanter's nightshade. It's over too soon and the busy road brings a rude awakening but you could always go round again.

the walk

1 In the middle of the lay-by there's a **stile and gate** into the corner of a field. Go up the side of the field and left along the top, then into a wood. Cross a small footbridge and continue up the footpath, then alongside a tiny **stream**. Follow the side of a **conifer plantation** until it bends

An overgrown woodland path at Fairy Glen

away, then bear right to the left-hand side of a clump of trees enclosing a **pool**. Continue up to the right into an enclosed track below **power lines** and on up to a junction with a tarmac track.

2 Go left, then bear left again down an **earthy track**. (To visit the Rigbye Arms first, go right at this point, then left along High Moor Lane. Retrace the route.) At the end of the earthy track go slightly right, across a field, to the corner of a **wood** then down its left-hand edge. Keep following this, which eventually becomes a narrow strip of **woodland**, to a stile in the bottom corner of the field. Follow a footpath down through the wood and then up to the A5209.

3 Cross the road and go left to a stile where the pavement ends. Go straight down a field and over another stile into a lane. Go right on this then immediately left down another lane. Cross the railway at a level crossing and continue until you reach a bridge. Drop down to the **tow path** and follow it eastwards for about a 0.5 mile (800m) to the next canal bridge (**No 40**).

WALK

Douglas Valley

LANCASHIRE

2h00 — 4 MILES — 6.4 KM — LEVEL 1 2 3

MAP: OS Explorer 285 Southport & Chorley
START/FINISH: Large lay-by on A5209 west of Parbold; grid ref: SD 517109
PATHS: field paths and canal tow path, 11 stiles
LANDSCAPE: open fields, enclosed valley and wooded dell
PUBLIC TOILETS: none on route
TOURIST INFORMATION: Preston, tel 01772 253731
THE PUB: The Rigbye Arms, Wrightington

Getting to the start

This walk is equidistant from Wrightington and Parbold, about 3 miles (5km) west of Standish. The start of the walk is also accessible by public transport, which operates along the A5209.

Researched and written by:
Terry Marsh, Jon Sparks

View from Parbold Hill across fields and rolling countryside

what to look for

A conspicuous plant, of the canal banks in particular, is Indian (or Himalayan) balsam. It has reddish stems and, from July to October, showy white to pink flowers. Even more conspicuous, in a few places, is giant hogweed. It can grow anywhere up to 15ft (5m) tall and touching its hairy stems or leaves can lead to a severe skin irritation. Both species were introduced to Britain in the 19th century.

Where the track finally parts company go ahead over a stile and along the bottom edge of a field. Cross the next field to a post and then a stile.

5 Descend the steep steps down into a wood and bear left into **Fairy Glen**. Cross a footbridge, climb some steps, then go left along a good track. Cross another footbridge below a **waterfall** and ascend more steps. Keep to the principal footpath, straight on up the glen as it becomes much shallower, until the path crosses a tiny **footbridge**. Soon after this the footpath leaves the side of the brook and briefly joins a track before it emerges on to the **A5209**. Cross and go right, back to the lay-by.

4 Cross this bridge and follow an obvious track, taking you back over the **railway** and up to a gate. Turn right on another track. In two places there's a separate footpath alongside, but it's always obvious.

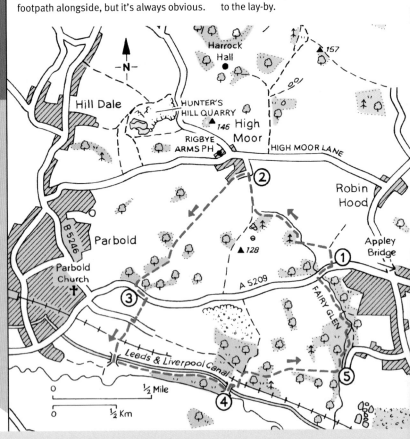

The Rigbye Arms

A perennial favourite among local ramblers, this 16th-century inn enjoys a remote moorland setting and provides a relaxed atmosphere and a warming open fire in the rambling, traditionally furnished interior. Muddy boots will be most at home in the Fox Hole Bar at the back. Here you'll find hand-pumped ales and popular, generously served food, ranging from pub favourites to more imaginative specials. Good outdoor seating for fine weather drinking, the garden features a barbeque and a Crown Bowling Green!

Food

Tuck into hearty sandwiches and traditional pub dishes, or look to the specials board for 'man-sized' steak and kidney pudding, freshly battered cod, chips and mushy peas, or braised lamb served with huge portions of vegetables.

Family facilities

Families are genuinely welcomed and there are family dining areas, a children's menu and a play area in the garden.

Alternative refreshment stops

On High Moor Lane you'll find the High Moor Inn, while near by you could seek out the Eagle & Child at Bispham Green or the Mulberry Tree at Wrightington Bar as both offer excellent food.

☛ Where to go from here

Visit Martin Mere, one of Britain's most important wetland sites, and get really close to a variety of ducks, geese and swans (www.wwt.org.uk). Take a look at Rufford Old Hall, built in 1530 and containing a fine collection of tapestries, arms, armour, and Tudor and Jacobean furniture (www.nationaltrust.org.uk). Children will love the Camelot Theme Park with its thrilling rides and spectacular shows (www.camelotthemepark.co.uk).

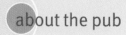

about the pub

The Rigbye Arms
2 Whittle Lane, Wrightington
Wigan, Lancashire WN6 9QB
Tel: 01257 462354

DIRECTIONS: off A5209 between Parbold and the M6 (J27) via Robin Hood Lane and High Moor Lane; see Point 2	
PARKING: 40	
OPEN: daily; all day Sunday	
FOOD: daily	
BREWERY/COMPANY: Tetley	
REAL ALE: Timothy Taylor Landlord, Tetley, Marston's Pedigree, guest beer	
DOGS: allowed in the Fox Hole Bar	

Burwardsley and Bulkeley Hill

A loop walk on a prominent sandstone ridge.

In Cheshire's sandstone country

Beeston Castle, visible from afar, was built in the 13th century. It saw no real battles until the Civil War and was largely demolished in 1646 on Parliament's orders. Nearby Peckforton Castle is a 19th-century imitation of a medieval fortress.

Distant views of these castle-crowned ridges might herald airy ridge walking but there's little of that to be found here, though Raw Head Hill does provide some drama. Generally, however, this walk delivers something different and equally pleasurable. The castles proclaim the long history of the area, but there is more history here. Coppermines Lane, at the start, is a reminder of an industrial element. Where the walk first leaves the tarmac, a chimney marks the site of the old copper works.

From here the way climbs to Raw Head Hill, along a steep slope which breaks into startling crags at Musket's Hole. The summit, is the highest point on the Sandstone Trail, a 34-mile (55km) route from Frodsham to Whitchurch. However, a screen of trees means it's far from the best viewpoint. The walk does serve up some great views, but never an all-round panorama.

After Raw Head Hill the walk winds down through woods, fields and a quiet lane to Burwardsley village and up an even

The quiet countryside around Burwardsley

quieter one to Higher Burwardsley. Then it climbs again to the National Trust-owned Bulkeley Hill Wood. The high point is a wonderful grove of sweet chestnut trees on a broad shelf rimmed by low sandstone crags. With virtually no undergrowth, you can fully appreciate the gnarled, multi-stemmed trees. From here it's an easy stroll back to Coppermines Lane.

the walk

1 Walk down **Coppermines Lane** to a sharp left-hand bend then over a stile beside an arched sandstone overhang. Bear right through bracken then ascend the edge of a wooded area. Cross fields to the edge of another wood. Go up right, joining a track towards **Chiflik Farm**.

2 Go through a kissing gate by the farm and up a fenced path. The path generally runs just below the top of a steep slope, gradually climbing to the trig point on **Raw Head Hill**.

3 The path goes right and into a slight dip. Go left down **steps** (leaving the Sandstone Trail) then back right, slanting through a **steep plantation**. Go left again down a narrow lane for 200yds (180m). At a footpath sign on the right, descend rightwards on clear ground under tall trees. At the bottom, cross a stile and go up

2h30   5.5 MILES   8.8 KM   LEVEL 2

MAP: OS Explorer 257 Crewe & Nantwich

START/FINISH: verges at end of tarmac on Coppermines Lane, off A534; grid ref: SJ 520550

PATHS: field and woodland paths, plus some lane walking, 9 stiles (currently being replaced by gates)

LANDSCAPES: richly varied woodland and farmland, some rocky outcrops and views over lush plains

PUBLIC TOILETS: none on route

TOURIST INFORMATION: Chester, tel 01244 402111

THE PUB: The Pheasant Inn, Higher Burwardsley

Getting to the start
Roughly mid-way between Tarporley and Malpas, Burwardsley and Higher Burwardsley lie west of the wooded Peckforton Hills amid a tangle of country lanes.

Researched and written by:
Terry Marsh, Jon Sparks

Burwardsley

CHESHIRE

Looking for miles across the Cheshire Plain to a distant horizon

towards **Bodnook Cottage**. Just below this bear left and into a **wood**. Follow a much clearer path, roughly level then slightly left and downhill among spindly beech trees.

4 Cross a stile at the edge of the wood, then another immediately to its right. Follow a narrow path to a stile below a large tree, 50yds (46m) left of a house. The path is clearer through the next field. At the end, cross a stile and follow the road ahead.

5 On the edge of **Burwardsley village** turn right up the first lane (Church Road). Go right again up **Sarra Lane**, then fork left at an 'Unsuitable for Motor Vehicles' sign. Follow the lane through a narrow section

then past **Cheshire Workshops**. Just opposite the car park entrance the road forks.

6 Go right to a **crossroads**; Rock Lane opposite. **The Pheasant Inn** is a short way down to the left, just round a corner on the right. Return to **Rock Lane** and turn into it. Keep right at the next fork. The lane becomes unsurfaced at the Crewe and Nantwich boundary.

7 On reaching the boundary sign go right through a **kissing gate** and follow a clear path down the edge of a field. Keep straight on until you meet a narrow lane and go up left. On the crest, opposite a **gatehouse**, go right on a track.

8 Go left up steps into the **wood** and continue less steeply. Where the path splits, the left branch follows the brink of a steep slope. Keep fairly close to this edge as the path levels. Go through a gap in a fence then descend straight ahead, through a **plantation**, to a kissing gate alongside a big iron gate. Go diagonally right on a clear track across a field to **Coppermines Lane**.

what to look for

Sweet chestnuts, like those in Bulkeley Hill Wood, are not a native species; they probably arrived with the Romans. Nor are they closely related to the horse chestnut, which gets its name from the chance resemblance of its fruit. In fact the sweet chestnut is related to the oaks.

The Pheasant Inn

A delightful old sandstone inn, formerly a 17th-century farmhouse, tucked away in a beautiful rural setting with lofty views over the Cheshire Plain to Liverpool and North Wales – the tiered patio is a stunning spot from which to savour a pint of local Weetwood ale. This traditional country inn is cosy indoors, with the oldest, half-timbered part of the inn housing the smartly refurbished, wood-floored bar, which features the largest log fire in Cheshire, and there's a splendid stone-flagged conservatory dining room. A great setting for a bar that boasts sophisticated modern cooking and nine wines by the glass. The outbuildings have been tastefully converted to comfortable, individually decorated en suite bedrooms.

Food
Typically, begin with game terrine with gooseberry chutney, or wild mushroom risotto, move on to assiette of duck with confit of carrots and wild berry jus, fillet steak Rossini, and finish with warm chocolate pudding. Excellent lunchtime sandwiches and ploughman's.

Family facilities
The pub has a children's licence, so all ages are welcome throughout the pub. There's a children's menu, high chairs, baby-changing facilities, and play equipment in the garden.

Alternative refreshment stops
The Bickerton Poacher on the A534 near Coppermines Lane

☛ Where to go from here
Peckforton Castle isn't open to visitors, but Beeston Castle is – and to the elements too. Much of it is in ruins, apart from the gatehouse and some towers of the outer wall (www.english-heritage.org.uk). Its condition seems perfectly fitting for the atmospheric site. The romantic Gothic Cholmondeley Castle is surrounded by fine gardens with lakeside and woodland walks, and rare breeds of farm animals.

about the pub

The Pheasant Inn
Higher Burwardsley, Tattenhall
Cheshire CH3 9PF
Tel: 01829 770434
www.thepheasant-burwardsley.com

DIRECTIONS: from A41 Chester to Whitchurch road, turn left for Burwardsley and follow signs for the Cheshire Workshops

PARKING: 30

OPEN: daily; all day

FOOD: daily; all day Sunday

BREWERY/COMPANY: Free House

REAL ALES: Weetwood Best, Old Dog, Eastgate & Outhouse

DOGS: allowed in the garden only

ROOMS: 10 en suite

A circuit outside Frodsham

A short and simple walk on the crest and along the flanks of a prominent red sandstone escarpment.

Sandstone Trail

Frodsham is at the northern end of the Sandstone Trail. The sandstone ridge that bounds the western edge of the Cheshire Plain is not continuous but does dominate the lowlands along much of its length. In a few places it breaks out into real crags, notably at Beeston, Frodsham and Helsby.

On Woodhouse Hill, near the southern end of the circuit, there was once a hill fort, probably dating back to the Iron Age. It can be hard to discern the remains now, though it's easier if you go in the winter when they're less obscured by vegetation. After a steep descent the walk returns along the base of the scarp then climbs up through Dunsdale Hollow to the base of the crags. Here you can return to the crest by a flight

of steps, though there's an alternative for the adventurous in the steep scramble known to generations of Frodsham people as Jacob's Ladder. Above this the path passes more small crags, before emerging into the open at Mersey View, crowned by the village war memorial. As the name suggests, the grand curve of the Mersey is unmistakable. Hugging the nearer shore is the Manchester Ship Canal, joined almost directly below by the Weaver Navigation. Beyond it you can pick out Liverpool's airport and the city's two cathedrals.

the walk

1 Go right along the lane for 100yds (91m), then left down a sunken footpath and over a stile on to a **golf course**. The path is much older than the golf course and officially walkers have priority, but don't take it for granted! Head straight across and you'll arrive at the **17th tee**, where there's an arrow on a post. Drop down slightly to

Frodsham's war memorial

1h30	3 MILES	4.8 KM	LEVEL 1 2 3

WALK

MAP: OS Explorer 267 Northwich & Delamere Forest

START/FINISH: small car park on Beacon Hill, near Mersey View; grid ref: SJ 518766

PATHS: clear woodland paths, golf course, 4 stiles

LANDSCAPE: largely wooded steep slopes and gentler crest with a few open sections

PUBLIC TOILETS: in Frodsham village and at Castle Park

TOURIST INFORMATION: Runcorn, tel 01928 576776

THE PUB: The Ring O'Bells, Frodsham

Generally suitable for all ages; a steep descent at Jacob's Ladder means that children will need to be closely controlled on this section

Frodsham

CHESHIRE

Getting to the start

Frodsham, 2.5 miles (4km) south of Runcorn, and overlooking the Mersey Estuary, is easily reached from the M56 motorway and by rail (though it's quite a climb from the station to the start of the walk). The car park lies up a convoluted series of minor lanes, but it's easily figured out with the aid of a map.

Researched and written by:
Terry Marsh, Jon Sparks

the right, to a footpath into the trees right of a green. Bear left at a sign for Woodhouse Hill, down a few steps. Keep to the left, passing above crags, then go down steps into **Dunsdale Hollow**.

2 Go left, rising gently, below more **crags**. Pass a stile on the right then go up scratched steps on the corner of the rocks ahead. Follow a level path through trees, near the edge of the golf course. Soon after this ends, the path rises slightly and passes a **bench** and after another 20yds (18m), the path forks. Keep straight on along the level path, soon passing a **Woodland Trust sign**, to a wider clearing with a signpost on the left near the corner of a field beyond.

3 Just before the corner of the field there's a break in a very overgrown **low wall** on the right, from which a narrow

The view across Frodsham golf course towards Helsby

path slants steeply down the slope. There's some bare rock and it can be slippery when wet, so it needs a little care. Near the bottom it turns directly downhill to the bottom of the wood. From a **gate**, go right along the base of the hill. After 800yds (732m) the path twists and descends a little into the bottom of **Dunsdale Hollow**.

what to look for

New red sandstone is about 200 million years old which is fairly new in geological terms! It's a relatively soft rock, as you can see from the worn footholds of Jacob's Ladder. Curious knobbly shapes in some of the crags often result from wind erosion. Despite strenuous efforts at clearance, rhododendrons remain abundant in parts of the woods. Originating in the Himalayas, they are very hardy plants which frequently crowd out native species.

Cross this and go up the other side alongside a stone wall and up a flight of steps. Go right on a **sandy track**, climbing steadily then passing below a **steep rock face**.

4 Go left up steps, briefly rejoining the outward route. **Jacob's Ladder** is just to the left here, up the right-hand edge of the crags. When you reach the top, follow a sandy track, and then bear left at a signpost for **Mersey View**, with occasional Sandstone Trail markers, along the brink of the steeper slope. This passes below some small steep crags before emerging near the **war memorial**.

5 Turn right just at the memorial on a grassy footpath, aiming for **telecommunications towers** ahead. Go through the ornate **iron gates** on to the lane and turn right, back to the car park at the start of the walk.

F r o d s h a m   CHESHIRE

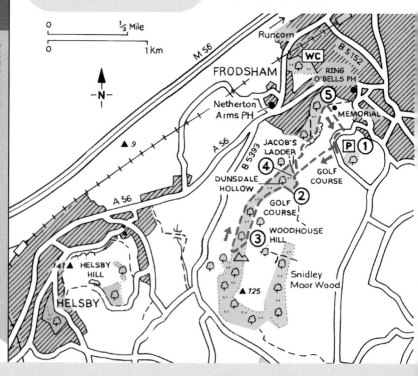

The Ring O'Bells

Rustic, white-painted 17th-century pub, festooned in summer with colourful hanging baskets, and pleasantly situated opposite the parish church. Three small, rambling rooms have antique settles, beams, dark oak panelling and stained glass, logs fires and lovely views over the church and the Mersey Plain. From a hatchway bar you can order pints of Black Sheep or the guest brew, and blackboard menus list some good-value lunchtime food. The secluded rear garden has a pond and plenty of shady trees for summer eating and drinking.

Food

Blackboards list sandwiches and filled baked potatoes and hearty walking fare such as steak and mushroom pie, Cumberland sausage and mash, and apple and blackberry crumble.

Family facilities

Children are welcome in the eating area of the bar only, where young children can choose from a standard children's menu.

Alternative refreshment stops

Also near the church in Frodsham is the Helter Skelter pub or you could try the Netherton Arms on the A56 between Frodsham and Helsby.

☛ Where to go from here

You can hardly ignore the chemical industry, especially from Mersey View, and you can find out a lot more about it at the Catalyst Science Discovery Centre near Widnes. Science and technology come alive through 100 interactive exhibits and hands-on displays (www.catalyst.org.uk). Just across the unmistakable Runcorn Bridge is Norton Priory Museum and Gardens (www.nortonpriory.org), where 38 acres (15.4ha) of peaceful woodland gardens provide the setting for the medieval priory remains, museum galleries and walled garden.

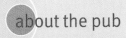

about the pub

The Ring O'Bells
Bellemont Road, Overton
Frodsham, Cheshire WA6 6BS
Tel: 01928 732068

DIRECTIONS:	off B5152 at parish church sign; pub opposite Overton church
PARKING:	20
OPEN:	daily
FOOD:	daily; lunchtime only
BREWERY/COMPANY:	Punch Taverns
REAL ALE:	two changing guest beers
DOGS:	allowed in the bar

Through Delamere Forest

CYCLE

Discover the wildlife of leafy Delamere Forest and its many trails.

Delamere Forest

Take time to have a look at Blakemere Moss, the largest of the peatlands in Delamere Forest Park, covering an area of roughly 82 acres (33ha). Peatlands are unique habitats lying somewhere between open water and dry land. The Moss started out as a water-filled hollow following the last ice age, about 11,000 years ago, created as the glacier, which covered this part of Cheshire, receded. The hollow was later colonised by plants which, as they died, sank to the bottom. However, because of the low levels of oxygen they did not decompose as plants normally do, but gradually built up layers of peat until they completely filled the hollow and created what we see today, a low-lying mire.

A gravel road through the Scots and Corsican pine trees in Delamere Forest Park

Delamere Forest woodland trail

1h30 · **7 MILES** · **11 KM** · **LEVEL 2**

MAP: OS Explorer 267 Northwich and Delamere Forest

START/FINISH: near the visitor centre at Linmere; grid ref: SJ 549705

TRAILS/TRACKS: good, stony, bumpy in places, generally dry

LANDSCAPE: woodland trails and tracks, waymarked throughout

PUBLIC TOILETS: at start

TOURIST INFORMATION: At start, and in Chester, tel 01244 402111

CYCLE HIRE: Eureka Cyclists cycle hire at the Visitor Centre, tel 0151 339 5629; www.eurekacyclists.co.uk

THE PUB: Abbey Arms, Oakmere

🛈 The route is undulating and some of the tracks are stony and uneven

Getting to the start
The nearest village is Hatchmere, about 4 miles (6.4km) south east of Frodsham. Head south from Hatchmere to Delamere Station, and there turn right to the Linmere car park. From the south, use the A49 from Tarporley, and then branch left onto the B5152 for Delamere.

Why do this cycle ride?
The ride provides an opportunity to explore a changing woodland landscape, one that is among the foremost places in Cheshire for birds and wildlife as it is far from major urban areas.

Researched and written by: Terry Marsh

The range of wildlife in the forest is exceptional. So, keep an eye open for a hunting fox, or a badger – though you'll be lucky to see either in broad daylight. But grey squirrels are plentiful. At dusk, you may spot noctule bats, darting among the trees. In daytime, see if you can pick out the call of the great tit – it sounds like it is calling 'Teacher, Teacher'. Patience may reward you with the sight of a treecreeper or a nuthatch. From a distance, they seem similar, but treecreepers invariably start at the bottom of trees and work their way up, while nuthatches often seem to hang upside down, and work their way down the tree.

the ride

1 Leave Linmere car park by riding left along the access road and shortly going left over a **railway bridge** onto a broad trail to a barrier. Beyond, continue along the trail. At the first major junction, near a **bench**, keep forward on the **white trail** – you follow the white trail throughout this ride. At the next junction, go left onto the

White Moor Trail, shortly bearing right. Cross a railway bridge onto a sandy track, and at the next junction, bear right again. The trail loops around and re-crosses the railway track to a junction. Go right to follow an undulating route through to a T-junction. Turn left, following the trail, which finally emerges at a roadway (**Ashton Road**).

2 Cross with care, and at the next two junctions, follow the **white trail**. At the next junction, stay with it, as it wheels right to follow another undulating stretch to a T-junction. Turn right, and then go through a dip at the bottom of which, when the trail forks, keep forward, climbing very steeply for a few moments to another junction.

3 Go forward, as the trail now twists and turns, and finally comes out to a T-junction, not far from Ashton Road.

4 Turn left, linking up with the **blue trail**. The route continues and once more crosses Ashton Road, on the other side heading down a **straight drive** through the forest. At the next junction, bear right, having now acquired the **red trail**. Keep on, with **Blakemere Moss** in view through the trees on the left. Before long the red trail diverts so continue with the blue and white trail to a T-junction, immediately at the edge of Blakemere Moss.

5 Turn right, and follow the trail as it bends around the end of the **lake**. At the next junction, keep forward for Linmere car park. Take the next track on the right to meet the outward trail at the **bench**. Bear left for the **visitor centre**, and retrace the outward route.

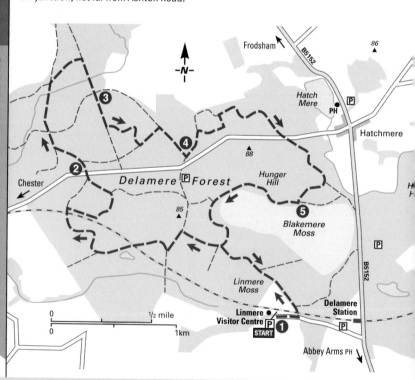

Abbey Arms

about the pub

Abbey Arms
Chester Road, Oakmere
Northwich, Cheshire CW8 2HB
Tel: 01606 882747

DIRECTIONS: return to Delamere Station
and the B5152 and turn right. The pub is at
the crossroads with the A556 in 2 miles
(3.2km)

PARKING: 100

OPEN: daily; all day

FOOD: daily; all day

BREWERY/COMPANY: Greene King

REAL ALE: Greene King IPA & Abbot Ale,
Ruddles, John Smiths Cask

*Children will love the Abbey Arms, so it's
well worth loading up the bikes after this
woodland ride for the 2 mile (3.2km)
drive to Oakmere. Owners Greene King
have invested heavily in providing
attractions for families, so much so that
kids won't want to leave. While dad and
mum savour a well-earned drink,
children will be content to explore the
huge adventure play area or have fun
at the crazy golf (free). If you're lucky,
your visit may coincide with the balloon
modeller and face-painting activity, both
monthly and free. At weekends there's
a tuck shop for children. This may be a
big, bright and breezy pub, but it has
a friendly, bustling atmosphere and
children will have a great time here.*

Food

A wide-ranging menu lists straightforward
pub food, from sandwiches to Tex-Mex
dishes, lamb kebabs, steak pie, curries, roast
chicken and a range of steaks and grills.

Family facilities

In addition to the above, there are high
chairs, baby-changing facilities, a children's
menu, and plenty of outdoor seating.

Alternative refreshment stops

None on the route. Kelsall has a range of
restaurants.

☞ Where to go from here

Spend some time exploring the city of
Chester. The cathedral, founded as a
Benedictine monastery in 1092, dates
from 1541 and is a fine example of a
medieval monastic complex
(www.chestercathedral.com). At the Dewa
Roman Experience discover what life was
like in Roman Britain through a
reconstructed street and the sights,
sounds and smells of Roman Chester.
Alternatively, visit Mouldsworth
Motor Museum.

CYCLE

Willington

CHESHIRE

11

Around Willington, Utkinton and Kelsall

Vistas of the lush Cheshire countryside.

Deer sheltering from the bright sunshine under a tree in a field at Willington

Fruity traditions

The village of Willington has a long tradition of fruit growing, so keep an eye open for fields of rhubarb or strawberries, as well as apple orchards and wild damson trees in the hedgerows. Damsons, normally associated with pies and jams, were also used to provide a dye for clothing and to add to whitewash to create pastel colours for room decoration. You may also spot some deer in a large park beside the route.

1h30	7 MILES	11 KM	LEVEL 123

MAP: OS Explorer 267 Northwich and Delamere Forest

START/FINISH: Chapel Lane, Willington; grid ref: SJ 531667

TRAILS/TRACKS: entirely on quiet country lanes, but with numerous ascents and descents

LANDSCAPE: mainly farmland

PUBLIC TOILETS: none on route

TOURIST INFORMATION: Chester, tel 01244 402111

CYCLE HIRE: Eureka Cyclists Cycle Hire, Woodbank, Chester, tel 0151 339 5629; www.eurekacyclists.co.uk

THE PUB: The Boot Inn, Boothsdale

🅛 Although fairly short this is an undulating ride on twisting and sometimes steep narrow lanes. Good road sense required

Getting to the start

Willington is one of many small villages in this part of rural Cheshire. The easiest approach is along the A54 Winsford to Tarvin road, or along the A556 from Northwich. An alternative is to head for Kelsall, and then by rural lanes to Willington. There is a small car park in Chapel Lane.

Why do this cycle ride?

This is a splendid exploration of pastoral Cheshire, following undulating and twisting lanes – care needed at all times against approaching traffic – and linking three charming villages. Cameo vistas of the lush Cheshire countryside come and go, seen through hedgerow gaps and from the top of country lanes.

Researched and written by: Terry Marsh

the ride

1 Leave the parking area in Chapel Lane and go left to **Willington Road,** turn left again. Follow the lane as it bends through a dip, and climbs gently flanked by hedgerows and woodland. At **Willington Hall Hotel,** turn left on a side road for **Utkinton,** climbing steeply. Soon you start to pass through **farmland**, bound for the village of Utkinton.

2 On reaching Utkinton, turn left into **Quarrybank**, now tackling a long, steep climb with good views on the right to distract from the effort. At the top of the climb, at the entrance to **Rowley Farm**, the road swings left. Keep following Quarrybank, still climbing, now more easily, and then beginning a long descent.

3 At a T-junction, go left, signed for **Kelsall**. Pass along the edge of **Primrosehill Wood**, a detachment from Delamere Forest mainly of Scots and Corsican pine, and continue towards Kelsall, before breaking out into farmland once more. Continue past the **Summer Trees Tea Shop**, and then take the next

turning on the right into **Waste Lane**. A long steady descent leads round a bend, and then go forward to the edge of Kelsall. At a crossroads, turn left, by **Th'ouse at Top pub** and follow the road round towards the centre of Kelsall.

4 Opposite the church, as the road bends to the right, turn left into **Church Street**. The road now descends to a T-junction. Go left into **Common Lane**, and then take the next left, signed for Willington and Utkinton. Now climb once more, past **farms** and large houses.

5 At the next junction turn right, for **Utkinton**. Go through a dip, passing the turning to **The Boot Inn**, and keep forward to complete the ride at Chapel Lane.

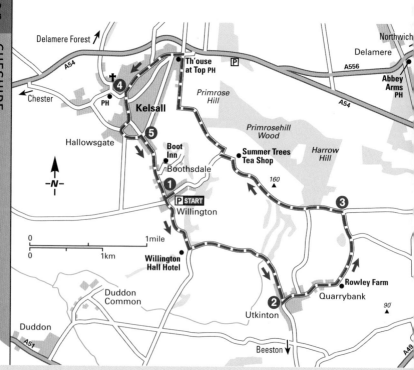

The Boot Inn

A real hidden gem in a superb setting on a wooded hillside, with views across the Cheshire plain to the Cllwydian hill, this quiet dining pub, originally a small ale house, has been converted from a charming row of sandstone cottages. Inside, it has been opened up, but you will find quarry-tiled floors, old beams, crackling log fires, and plenty of cosy alcoves around the central bar. An extension with French windows overlooks the small, sun-trap garden. The Boot offers tip-top ales – try the local Weetwood brews – decent wines and freshly prepared food.

Food

You're spoiled for choice if you fancy a hearty snack, as there are home-made soups with crusty bread, hot paninis, sandwiches (beef and horseradish), salad platters and hot baguettes filled with pork and peppers with hoisin sauce. Main meals take in braised shoulder of lamb with root vegetables and red wine, breast of duck with orange and cranberry, and smoked haddock with rarebit topping.

Family facilities

Although there are no special facilities for children, there is a family dining area and smaller portions of the main menu dishes can be ordered.

Alternative refreshment stop

Summer Trees Tea Shop on the route. Pubs and restaurants in Kelsall.

☞ Where to go from here

Children will enjoy a visit to Chester Zoo, the largest zoological gardens in Britain, with 7,000 animals and 500 species. Look for the penguin pool, the Bat Cave for endangered bat species, the National Elephant Centre, and the children's Fun Ark (www.chesterzoo.org). At Beeston Castle there are 4,000 years of history to be discovered and breathtaking views from the Pennines to the mountains of Wales (www.english-heritage.org.uk).

about the pub

The Boot Inn
Boothsdale, Willington
Tarporley, Cheshire CW6 0NH
Tel: 01829 751375

DIRECTIONS: signposted left off the minor road south of Kelsall towards Willington. Near the end of the cycle ride

PARKING: 60

OPEN: daily; all day Saturday & Sunday

FOOD: daily; all day Saturday & Sunday

BREWERY/COMPANY: Pubmaster

REAL ALE: Tetley, Bass, Greene King IPA, Weetwood beers

Woods and heaths of Little Budworth

An easy walk centred around the distinctive heathland of Little Budworth Country Park.

Budworth Country Park

In the middle of all the rich green farmland of lowland Cheshire is an island of a rougher, older landscape. Usually it's peaceful, but a word of warning – it is very close to the Oulton Park motor-racing circuit. On race days the traffic and noise are abominable.

The area now called Little Budworth Country Park is a fragment of lowland heath. Britain now has only 18 per cent of the area of lowland heath recorded in 1800.

The essence of heath is an open landscape, with a mix of heather, gorse, bracken and grasses and with only scattered, if any, trees. There are two characteristic species of heather: ling (*Calluna vulgaris*) and bell heather (*Erica cinerea*). They often grow together and look quite similar, but ling has slightly paler and more open flowers. Heathland typically developed in areas cleared of trees from Neolithic times onward, as the poor soil made it unsuitable for cultivation. The land was, however, used for grazing. Gorse was traditionally used as fuel and for animal fodder, while bracken provided animal bedding and was also a valuable source of potash. These activities, and the occasional natural fire, prevented the heath reverting to woodland. Much of today's country park is wooded, but you will also see large areas of heath.

The majority of the heathland at Little Budworth is dry, but there are some low-lying wetter areas. The pool passed on the walk is a breeding ground for dragonflies and damselflies. The second half of the walk crosses farmland and skirts Budworth Mere. Many of Cheshire's meres were created by subsidence resulting from salt mining. Others, like this one, are natural, formed in hollows left by retreating ice at the end of the last ice age.

Finally the walk visits Little Budworth village. It is peaceful and attractive but has not become a tourist magnet. You'll probably agree that this is to its benefit.

the walk

1 Go straight across the **Coach Road** to a path then turn right on a wider path. Fork left and follow the main path, keeping straight on at a cross-path with a **Heathland Trail sign**, and again at the next crossing. When a field appears ahead, follow the path alongside to its right. This veers away right. Go back left just before a cleared area, by another Heathland Trail marker.

2 Go right on a wide track to the Coach Road and straight across into **Beech Road**. After 100yds (91m) go right on a path near a **metal barrier** to a former car park. Near its far end is a signboard with a map. Go through a gap in the fence beside this. The path skirts a depression with a **boggy pool**, then curves round a larger pool.

3 Cross a **causeway** by the pool and gently climb a sunken track beyond. As it levels out, fork left by a **Heathland Trail sign** then turn left, with an open field not far away to the left. Bear left on a wider surfaced track, swinging down past an **ornamental pool** in a dip. Immediately after this turn right on a sandy track beside a stream.

Preparations for a celebration in the village of Little Budworth

4 Where another path crosses, most people evidently go through a gate ahead into the corner of a field. Strictly speaking, however, the right of way goes over a **stile** to its right then across the very wet corner of a wood to a second stile close by. Over this, bear right under power lines, to a stile in the far corner. Follow a narrow path (beware nettles), then go over a stile on the right and straight across a large field. Aim just left of the **farm** to a gate and stile. Go left on a lane for 30yds (27m) then right down a track. This becomes narrower, then descends slightly.

5 As it levels out, there's a stile on the right, with a sign for **Budworth Mere**. Go down towards the water then left on a path skirting the mere. At the end go right

The countryside surrounding Little Budworth

1h30 — **3.5 MILES** — **5.7 KM** — **LEVEL 1**23

MAP: OS Explorer 267 Northwich & Delamere Forest

START/FINISH: main car park for Little Budworth Country Park; grid ref: SJ 590654

PATHS: easy tracks at first, field paths and some (usually quiet) road walking, 9 stiles

LANDSCAPE: mature woodland, open heath, farmland and mere

PUBLIC TOILETS: at start

TOURIST INFORMATION: Northwich, tel 01606 353534

THE PUB: Red Lion Inn, Little Budworth

Getting to the start

Little Budworth is a small village 2.5 miles (4km) west of Winsford and 3 miles (4.8km) north east of Tarporley in the area of Cheshire known as Vale Royal.

Researched and written by:
Terry Marsh, Jon Sparks

up a road, swinging further right into the centre of **Little Budworth**, passing the Red Lion pub.

6 Keep straight on along the road, through the village then past open fields, and passing **Park Road**. Opposite the main entrance gates of **Oulton Park** is the start of the **Coach Road**. Follow this, or the parallel footpath to its left for 125yds (114m), to the car park.

what to look for

The Heathland Trail signs show a great spotted woodpecker, though ironically this is (as you'd imagine) a woodland bird. A characteristic bird of the true heath is the stonechat. The males are easily recognised with black heads, white collars and orange breasts. Both sexes make a distinctive sound, like two pebbles being knocked together.

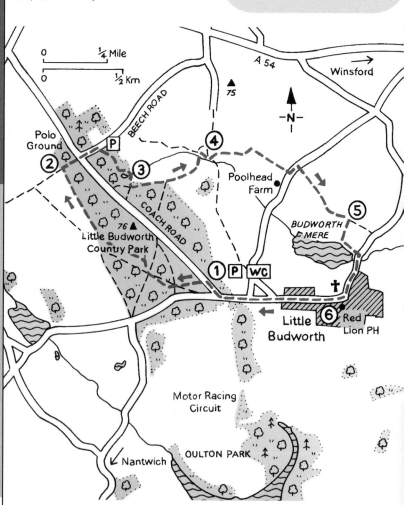

Red Lion Inn

Formerly a coaching inn dating from 1797, the Red Lion is a small, friendly village pub in an unspoiled rural spot, with original oak beams, ancient settles, winter log fires, and gleaming copper and brassware. You'll also find Robinson's ales on tap and good bar food at very reasonable prices. There's outside seating at the front, close to the road – but the traffic's light – and more benches and umbrellas at the back, overlooking the bowling green.

Food

As well as the usual bar snacks like soup, sandwiches and pub favourites, there's pork fillet, pan-fried chicken, salmon Provence, and grilled gammon steak.

Family facilities

Children are welcome in the family dining area if eating. There's a simple children's menu and smaller portions of the menu are available.

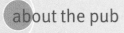

about the pub

Red Lion Inn

Vicarage Lane, Little Budworth
Tarporley, Cheshire CW6 9BY
Tel: 01829 760275

DIRECTIONS: see Getting to the start; pub in the village centre opposite the church

PARKING: 30

OPEN: all day; closed Monday

FOOD: daily

BREWERY/COMPANY: Robinsons Brewery

REAL ALE: Robinsons beers, guest beers

DOGS: allowed in the garden only

ROOMS: 4 en suite

Alternative refreshment stops

The Egerton Arms in Budworth, or the Abbey Arms near Delamere.

☞ Where to go from here

Nearby Northwich, like Middlewich and Nantwich, prospered on salt and Britain's only Salt Museum tells the story of Cheshire's oldest industry. Much of Northwich was rebuilt after a catastrophic fire in 1583 though 14th-century St Mary's Church, one of the finest in Cheshire, survived. Churche's Mansion is an impressive Tudor house. Just outside Nantwich, Stapeley Water Gardens is the world's largest Water Garden Centre and the Palms Tropical Oasis is home to exotic flowers and a zoo collection (www.stapeleywg.com).

Goosnargh and Beacon Fell Country Park

Ride the lanes of Lancashire to the top of wooded Beacon Fell.

Sculpture Trail

From the Visitor Centre on Beacon Fell there is a Sculpture Trail, featuring the work of local artist Thompson Dagnall, which uses materials found locally. Along the way you might find a serpent and, near the top of the fell, a bat hidden in the trees. All these are wooden, of course, but the country park is a remarkable habitat, and you should keep eyes and ears open for chaffinch, willow warbler, goldcrest, bullfinch, siskin and the occasional crossbill. Rabbits and hares are plentiful, too, and easily spotted in the bushes and the surrounding farm fields. Not surprisingly, they tend to be timid, as the sky here is patrolled by kestrels, sparrowhawk and tawny owls on the lookout for a ready meal, and stoat, weasel and fox are not above a rabbit lunch.

The view from Beacon Fell across the Bowland Fells

the ride

1 Begin past **Bushell House** and immediately turn left into **Mill Lane**, a narrow lane flanked by hedgerows, climbing gently, and continuing past houses out into a more rural setting, and later descending through a dip to cross a bridge. Go past the end of **Broadith Lane**, and keep forward passing Curwen Lane, and remaining on Mill Lane to pass through a tunnel of trees to a crossroads.

2 Keep forward into **Syke House Lane**, with Beacon Fell soon coming into view. Stay on the main road, passing Church Lane and Bullsnape Lane, and, just after passing **Back Lane**, descend gently through bends into a dip and out through a lightly wooded stretch. Turn left for **Beacon Fell Country Park**, into Barns Lane.

3 When the road makes a pronounced right-hand bend, go left into **Carwags Lane**, leaving the main road for a very

Looking back towards Beacon Fell

MAP: OS Explorer 286 Blackpool and Preston and OL41 Forest of Bowland and Ribblesdale

START/FINISH: Public parking adjacent to the church in Goosnargh; grid ref: SD 559369

TRAILS/TRACKS: entirely on country lanes, some very narrow with high hedgerows

LANDSCAPE: rolling farmland

PUBLIC TOILETS: none on route

TOURIST INFORMATION: Clitheroe, tel: 01200 425566

CYCLE HIRE: Pedal Power, Waddington Road, Clitheroe, Lancashire BB7 2HJ, tel 01200 422066

THE PUB: Bushells Arms, Goosnargh

🛈 There is a very long but steady ascent up to Beacon Fell and around its circular route, followed by equally long and steady descents

Getting to the start

Goosnargh lies about 5 miles (8km) north east of Preston, and is easily reached via M6 (Jct 32) and M55 (Jct 1), north on A6 to Broughton, and then right to Goosnargh. At the post office, turn left into Church Lane, and follow this north to the start.

Why do this cycle ride?

Beacon Fell Country Park is an isolated hill rising to 873ft (266m), on the edge of the Bowland Fells. It is an area of rough moorland and woodland within the Forest of Bowland Area of Outstanding Natural Beauty, and was one of the first designated country parks in Britain. There are tremendous views north and south from the highest ground, and the approach along country lanes displays rural Lancashire at its very best.

Researched and written by: Terry Marsh

narrow lane, and a very long and steady climb, which young children may find tiring, up towards Beacon Fell. On reaching, **Beacon Fell Road**, go forward into a one-way system.

4 At the turning to **Crombleholme Fold** you need to make a decision. The circuit around Beacon Fell is delightful, but one-way: Crombleholme Fold is the continuing route, but a short way beyond the junction lies the **Bowland Visitor Centre**, toilets, café and information point. Once you pass Crombleholme Fold, you are committed to cycling all the way around the fell, with still more ascent on the northern side. Cycling within the woodland is permitted, but only on surfaced tracks. If you go around the fell – recommended – you will be treated to lovely views northwards to the **Bowland Fells,** and in due course return to the Crombleholme Fold turning. Turn left, descending steeply. At a T-junction, turn left into **Bleasdale Road**, and shortly left again into **Button Street**.

5 Follow a hedgerowed lane into the village of **Inglewhite**. Go past the village green to a crossroads, and keep forward into **Silk Mill Lane**, which gradually descends to cross **Sparting Brook**, climbing steadily on the other side. At a T-junction, turn right onto **Langley Lane** (signed for Preston).

6 Go through two S-bends, followed by a long, more or less straight and level section to a pronounced left bend (occasional flooding here), that leads down to a **hump bridge**, and a short climb beyond. Continue as far as **Goosnargh Lane**, and there turn left to return to **Goosnargh village**.

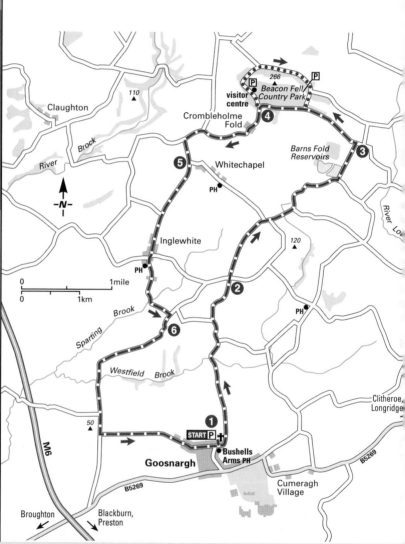

Bushells Arms

Dr Bushell was a philanthropic Georgian who built his villagers not just a hospital, but this pub too. And he chose a lovely spot, beside the village green and overlooking the parish church. Expect a congenial and relaxing atmosphere in the cosy beamed bar, where you will find leather armchairs and a log fire in the stone fireplace. There's also an intimate, candlelit restaurant.

Food

For a light bite peruse the hot and cold sandwich menus. For something more substantial tuck into ham hock on minted pea and potato cake, pork loin with black pudding and a white onion sauce, beer battered cod, the Bushell burger with pepper sauce and hand-cut chips, or, naturally, the renowned roasted Goosnargh duckling with apple sauce.

Family facilities

Families are welcome and smaller portions from the main menu can be provided for children. Make use of the secluded rear garden on fine days, replete with flower borders and a spacious lawn.

Alternative refreshment stops

Café, picnic and barbecue sites in the country park, plus pubs in Goosnargh.

☛ Where to go from here

Visit the ancient market town of Clitheroe and explore the town's 12th-century castle. The Castle Museum brings to life the history and geology of the Ribble Valley. At the National Football Museum in Preston you can take a fascinating trip through football past and present. There's a fine display of memorabilia, interactive displays that allow visitors to commentate on matches, and virtual trips to every League ground in the country. (www.nationalfootballmuseum.com).

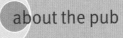

about the pub

Bushells Arms

Church Lane, Goosnargh
Preston, Lancashire PR3 2BH
Tel: 01772 865235

DIRECTIONS: see Getting to the start
PARKING: use public car park opposite
OPEN: all day; closed Monday except Bank Holidays
FOOD: daily; all day Sunday
BREWERY/COMPANY: Enterprise Inns
REAL ALE: Marston's Pedigree, Timothy Taylor Landlord, Black Sheep Bitter, Tetley, guest beers

Rocks and water at Anglezarke

WALK

A landscape shaped by
quarries and reservoirs,
full of both historical
and natural interest.

Anglezarke Quarry

A string of reservoirs moats the western
side of the high moors of Anglezarke and
Rivington and quarries scar their flanks.
This is not a pristine landscape by any
stretch of the imagination, yet today it is
seen by many as an oasis of tranquillity
close to busy towns and a motorway.

A gentle start just above the shores of
Anglezarke Reservoir leads to Lester Mill
Quarry, which was worked until the 1930s.
The quarry wall is imposing, but somewhat
vegetated, and the rock is loose in places.
It is much less popular with climbers than
Anglezarke Quarry.

The route continues through a mix of
woodland and pasture to the head of the
lake, then heads up the valley below steep,
bouldery Stronstrey Bank. There's another
quarry high on the right near the end of the
bank, seemingly guarded by a number of
gaunt, dead trees. Just beyond is another,
set further back. Just beyond this, an
impressive spillway testifies to the
potential power of Dean Black Brook.

Now you cross The Goit, a canal that
feeds the reservoir, to White Coppice
cricket ground. There's a small reservoir
just above and you pass others on the
way down to the present-day hamlet.
These served the mills that flourished
here for well over a century. Along with
the quarries at Stronstrey Bank these
made White Coppice a busy industrial
village with a population that may have
approached 200. The mill closed in 1914
and little remains.

After White Coppice you climb to
Healey Nab. Trees obscure what must have
been a fine all-round view from the highest
point, but there's a good southward
prospect from the large cairn on Grey
Heights. Winter Hill is the highest of the
moors, unmistakable with its TV towers. The
main mast is just over 1,000ft (305m) tall,
so you could argue that its tip is the highest
point in Lancashire. The string of reservoirs
is also well displayed and you get a bird's-
eye view of Chorley.

the walk

1 Leave the car park and go back down
the **access road** to a kissing gate on the
right and follow a track near the water. Fork
right, on a side path that leads through
Lester Mill Quarry. On rejoining the original
path, turn right. The track soon begins to
climb along the edge of **woodland**.

2 As the track bends right, go through
a gap on the left. The path traverses a
wooded slope. Descend steps, join a wider
track and go left. Beyond a kissing gate
follow a narrower path until it meets a road.

3 Go left 25yds (20m) to a kissing gate.
Follow a track up the valley below
Stronstrey Bank. Cross a bridge then go
through a kissing gate and over another
bridge to **White Coppice cricket ground**.

4 Bear left up a lane, then follow tarmac
into **White Coppice** hamlet. Cross a
bridge by the postbox. Follow a stream,
then go up left by a **reservoir**. Bear left to

a stile. Cross the next field to its top right corner and go right on a lane. Where it bends right go left up a track.

5 Skirt **Higher Healey**, follow hedged track, then angle up left into **dark plantations**. Fork left just inside, and ascend to an **old quarry** and follow its rim to enter a larch plantation.

6 Go forward to meet a clear path on the far side of the **plantation**. Turn left and immediately right to the large cairn on **Grey Heights**. Descend slightly right, winding down through gorse and past a **small plantation**. Below the plantation, bear left between hedgerows, cross two fences then follow a rough field track to a lane by **White House Farm**.

7 Cross a stile on the left below the **farmyard wall,** then bear left to the

2h30 — **7 MILES** **11.3 KM** **LEVEL 1 2 3**

14

WALK

Anglezarke

LANCASHIRE

MAP: OS Explorer 287 West Pennine Moors

START/FINISH: Large car park at Anglezarke; grid ref: SD 621161

PATHS: mostly good tracks with some field paths, 10 stiles

LANDSCAPE: woodland, reservoirs, open valleys and farmland

PUBLIC TOILETS: none on route

TOURIST INFORMATION: Preston, tel 01772 253731

THE PUB: The Yew Tree, Dill Hall Brow

Getting to the start

Anglezarke and its reservoirs lie in the shadow of Winter Hill just 2 miles (3.2km) to the east of Chorley and reached via minor roads from the A6 in Chorley or the A673 at Adlington.

Researched and written by:
Terry Marsh, Jon Sparks

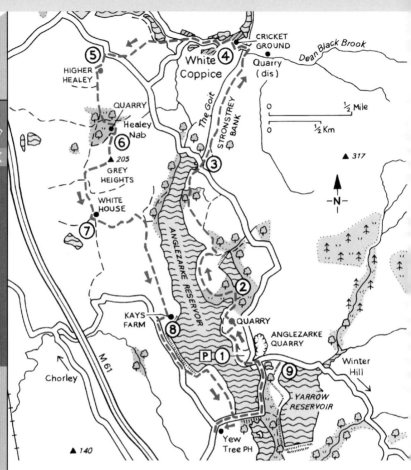

corner of the field. Cross the stile on the left, then along the field edge to stile on right, and join a confined path to a stile on the right. Follow trees along the field edge to a rough track. Go right and straight on to **Kays Farm**.

8 Go right down a track then left on a lane below the **reservoir wall**. As the lane angles away, go left over a stile then skirt the reservoir until pushed away from the water by a wood. Join the road across the **dam**.

9 To visit **The Yew Tree**, turn right and follow the road. Retrace your steps, and continue across the dam, following the road back to the car park.

what to look for

Subtle differences in the nature of the rock can be seen in the different quarries. These were significant for the uses to which the stone could be put. Parts of Anglezarke Quarry are 'massive' – there are very few cracks. Some of the rock here is especially pure and was used to line blast furnaces.

The Yew Tree

The Yew Tree, at Lane Ends, 250yds (229m) from the Anglezarke dam, may lack cask beer but offers a lovely moorland location on the edge of the West Pennine Moors, extensive views and a cosy atmosphere. Although very much a pub-restaurant, with a big emphasis on food, it does have a bar, serves light bar meals and, more importantly, welcomes walkers. Benches in the garden make the most of the views.

Food

Lunchtime bar meals may include roast ham, beef, or tuna mayonnaise sandwiches, Spanish omelette, grilled gammon, pasta bake, fresh haddock and plaice, steak pie and liver, onions and mash. The restaurant menu takes in halibut Breton, whole plaice and rack of lamb.

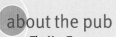

about the pub

The Yew Tree
Dill Hall Brow, Heath Charnock, Chorley,
Lancashire PR6 9HA
Tel: 01257 480344

DIRECTIONS: see Getting to the start; pub at the southern end of Anglezarke Reservoir and best accessed from the A673 at Adlington south of Chorley; see Point **9**	
PARKING: 75	
OPEN: daily; all day Sunday	
FOOD: daily; all day Sunday	
BREWERY/COMPANY: Free House	
REAL ALE: none served	
DOGS: allowed in the garden only	

Family facilities
Families are welcome inside but there are no special facilities for children.

Alternative refreshment stops
North of White Coppice just off the A674 at Wheelton (Briers Brow) is the Dressers Arms (excellent beer and locally sourced food), and beside the canal at Heapey is the Top Lock offering traditional pub food.

☛ Where to go from here
Enter King Arthur's Kingdom at the Camelot Theme Park for a magical day out watching spectacular shows, including a jousting tournament, and enjoy some of the thrilling rides (www.camelotthemepark.co.uk). Visit Astley Hall, a 400-year-old mansion with fine architecture and ornate furnishings, set in a scenic country park south of Chorley (www.lancashiretourism.com).

Cuerden Valley to Preston and back

Discover Chorley's best-kept secret, the valley of the River Lostock.

Flora & fauna

Most of Cuerden's 700 acres (284ha) are actively farmed, providing changing scenes throughout the year. The Valley Park is home to foxes, grey squirrels, great-spotted and green woodpeckers, patrolling buzzards and the occasional sparrowhawk, as well as a host of smaller birds, up to 70 species in all. The Preston Junction Nature Reserve, north of Bamber Bridge, is a good place to spot butterflies – common blue, small copper, meadow brown, wall brown,

gatekeeper, orange tip small tortoiseshell. There are also some attractive ponds along this stretch, bright in spring and summer with yellow waterlilies. The reserve was built around the trackbed of the old Preston tramway.

Cuerden Hall is owned by the Sue Ryder Foundation and houses a small cafeteria; it is off-route, but easily accessible by turning left on reaching the A49 (rather than the route continuation, which goes right).

the ride

1 Leave the car park and immediately turn left onto the **Cuerden Valley Cycle Route**. At a junction bear left onto a slightly narrower track, and continue onto a surfaced track, climbing a little and then going forward to meet a main road. Turn right for 120 yards (100m), and then turn left to rejoin the cycle route.

2 The route through the valley park follows a broad, clear track, at one point bending right and left to pass through the edge of woodland before rejoining the course of the River Lostock to a bridge, water splash (for the adventurous) and **picnic tables**. Off to the right, a short distance, at this point is the **park lake**, which is home to numerous waterbirds, including at some times of year more than 250 Canada geese. Cross the bridge and go right, climbing briefly but steeply to follow a field edge path to a **bridge** spanning the M6 motorway, beyond which you descend to a car park and the A49.

3 Turn right on a **cycle lane** to a light-controlled crossing of the A6 at **Bamber**

Left: Cuerden Hall
Below left: Preston Junction Nature Reserve

2h30 · **13 MILES** · **20 KM** · **LEVEL 1** 23

MAP: OS Explorer 286 Blackpool and Preston

START/FINISH: Whittle-le-Woods, Chorley, down Factory Lane; grid ref: SD 575217

TRAILS/TRACKS: good tracks, stony in places, or surfaced

LANDSCAPE: river valley park, small urban section, woodland

PUBLIC TOILETS: none on route

TOURIST INFORMATION: Chorley, tel 01257 241693

CYCLE HIRE: none locally

THE PUB: Halfway House Hotel, Clayton-le-Woods

Getting to the start

Whittle-le-Woods is a suburb of Chorley, and lies along the A6, 2 miles (3.2km) north of the town. The start of the Cuerden Cycle Route is down Factory Lane in Whittle-le-Woods, just to the north of the church.

Why do this cycle ride?

Long stretches of traffic-free cycling through a wooded river valley are linked by safe cycling crossing points and cycle lanes into an old railway trackbed and then an even older tramway trackbed into city centre parks in Preston. The whole ride is through an intense area of habitat for a diverse range of flora and fauna. The ride can be shortened by taking a picnic as far as the bridge crossing in Cuerden Valley Park.

Researched and written by: Terry Marsh

Bridge. Go forward, still on a cycle lane, as far as **Church Road**, and there cross the road at a safe crossing point, and turn into **Havelock Road**. Follow the road, shortly passing a small **industrial estate** to meet another lane. Turn right, and go past a **supermarket** car park, turning right onto a cycle lane once more, and through a low **tunnel** (dismount here). Just beyond, turn left beneath a road bridge into the edge of a housing estate. At a T-junction turn right towards a roundabout, but cross, left, just before it to enter the **Preston Junction Local Nature Reserve**.

4 Follow a clear track to a road. Cross and keep forward to cross another back lane. Go forward along the middle one of three possibilities. After a short rise the towers of **Preston** come into view. Descend to cross a farm access track, and keep on to meet a gravel track along the edge of **woodland**.

5 When the gravel track forks, branch right, descending to a track junction beside the **River Ribble**. Turn right to the next bridge, and here bear right and left to gain the bridge, across which the **Miller and Avenham Parks** mark the end of the route. Across the parks the centre of Preston is soon reached.

6 Return by re-crossing the bridge, but instead of dipping down to the Ribble, keep forward along an **avenue of trees** to meet the back lane crossed on the way out. Here rejoin the outward route, and retrace this first to **Bamber Bridge** and, once safely over the A6, back into **Cuerden Valley Park** and on to Whittle-le-Woods.

CYCLE

Cuerden Valley   LANCASHIRE

Preston Station

Preston

A6

B6230

River Ribble

6

5

A675

M6

● Mains House Farm

River Darwen

Higher Walton

A6

Walton-le-Dale

B6258

Jct 30

Penwortham Lane

A6

Bamber Bridge

M61

B5254

4

B5257

Walton Summit

Tardy Gate

M65

Lostock

A6

River

A582

A6

P

Jct 29/1

M65

Cuerden Green

3

Clayton Brook

A6

A5083

M6

● Cuerden Hall

P

Clayton Green

Farington

Cuerden Valley Park

P

2

● Halfway House Hotel

M61

B5256

Jct 28

B5256

Clayton-le-Woods

Leyland

1

START P

✝ Whittle-le-Woods

B5248

A49

B5248

Worden Park

0 ———— 1mile

0 ———— 1km

Chorley ↓ A6

Halfway House Hotel

Reputedly at the exact 'halfway' point between London and Glasgow – hence its name – this modernised and comfortably refurbished roadside inn retains much of its former charm, when it was a favoured stopping point for charabancs bound for Blackpool and car travellers heading to and from Scotland. The traditionally furnished interior comprises a large lounge, dining room and a taproom with games area and the full range of Lees beers on tap. Note the lovely old sign on the gable entrance welcoming motorists and cyclists, a reminder of those early days of motoring and its time as a popular café for motorcyclists.

Food

Traditional pub food ranges from sausages and mash, pasta meals and lasagne to chargrilled pork chops and beef in black bean sauce. Sandwiches and light meals are also available.

Family facilities

Children can make good use of the outdoor play area in the beer garden on fine days. They are also welcome indoors and a children's menu is available.

Alternative refreshment stops

The ride passes near numerous restaurants, pubs and cafés in Preston and Chorley.

☛ Where to go from here

For a family fun outing that includes thrilling rides, jousting tournaments and spectacular magic shows, venture into King Arthur's Kingdom at Camelot Theme Park (www.camelotthemepark.co.uk) south of Leyland off the A49 near Charnock Richard.

about the pub

Halfway House Hotel
Preston Road, Clayton-le-Woods
Chorley, Lancashire PR6 7JB
Tel: 01772 334477

DIRECTIONS: beside the A6 a mile (1.6km) north of Factory Lane and the start of the ride	
PARKING: 100	
OPEN: daily; all day	
FOOD: daily; all day	
BREWERY/COMPANY: J W Lees Brewery	
REAL ALE: J W Lees Bitter, Moonraker & seasonal beers	
ROOMS: 36 en suite (adjoining Travel Lodge)	

Astley Hall west of Chorley is a charming Tudor/Stuart building set in beautiful parkland and retains a 'lived in' atmosphere. There are pictures and pottery to see, as well as fine furniture and rare plasterwork ceilings (www.lancashiretourism.com).

Around Rivington and its reservoir

Explore Lever Park and discover Lord Leverhulme's ruined castle.

Above: Rivington Reservoir

Castles and barns

Liverpool Castle is an intentional ruin, built on a small hill, Cob Lowe, by Lord Leverhulme as a replica of the castle in Liverpool Bay. It overlooks the waters of Lower Rivington Reservoir and has a fine view of Rivington Pike, one of Lancashire's best-known landmarks, one of a chain of beacon fires used to warn of danger. It was used at the time of the Spanish Armada in 1588.

Great House Barn is one of a small number of half-cruck barns in Lancashire, probably dating to Saxon times. Today it houses an information point, a gift shop

and tea room open every day of the year, except Christmas Day. Originally, it would have been used to shelter cattle and feed. From the barn an imposing driveway leads up to Rivington Hall, formerly the home of the Lord of the Manor. It has a fine red-brick Georgian façade, and, like the barns, was probably built on a site of Saxon importance.

the ride

1 Leave from the bottom end of the car park, passing a **barrier** and soon, at a track junction, turn left, descending to cross a narrow, **wooded gully**. Follow a clear track, around a field edge, to another track junction at the edge of large open area. Bear

right and follow a clear track to **Liverpool Castle**. From the castle entrance, head down a long woodland drive to meet a road.

2 Turn right for 330yds (300m), passing a **school**. At the end of **metal railings**, turn left up a surfaced lane to a rough stony track on left, the lowest of three tracks at this junction. Follow this along an avenue of trees to another track junction, and there turn right, pass a **gate** onto a gently rising track. Continue forward at the next gate. When the track forks, bear left, and curve round left and right to a rough-surfaced lane beside **Rivington Hall**. Bear right to ride behind the hall into a car park.

3 Cross the car park, go forward past a wooden barrier and down a **stony driveway**, the right-hand of two exit drives. When the drive forks, bear right to a road. Emerge with care and turn right to pass **Rivington Stocks**, and going left with the main road. On reaching **Upper Rivington Reservoir**, leave the road by turning right onto a narrow road (bridleway).

Rivington Hall, built in the 18th century, is passed on the cycle route

1h30 — **7.5 MILES** — **12 KM** — **LEVEL 2**

MAP: OS Explorer 19 West Pennine Moors

START/FINISH: Great House Barn car park, Rivington; grid ref: SD 628139

TRAILS/TRACKS: stony, woodland tracks and minor roads

LANDSCAPE: mainly woodland, some open areas around reservoirs

PUBLIC TOILETS: at start

TOURIST INFORMATION: Great House Barn (at the start)

CYCLE HIRE: none locally

THE PUB: The Millstone, Anderton

🛈 Some short ascents, and one long road climb

Getting to the start

Great House Barn lies within Lever Park, on the edge of Horwich. Accessible from Junction 8 on the M61 motorway, and then along the A6 through Chorley to Adlington on the A673, or from Junction 6, and then by A6027 and through Horwich on the A673.

Why do this cycle ride?

The wild uplands and string of reservoirs of the West Pennine Moors make fine habitats for flora and fauna alike, and provide a network of tracks, paths and trails for exploring. Lever Park, sometime property of Lord Leverhulme, where this ride begins, has at its centre the attractive village of Rivington and historical buildings like the Great House Barn, Rivington Hall and Liverpool Castle.

Researched and written by: Terry Marsh

CYCLE

Rivington

LANCASHIRE

4 Continue beside the reservoir (left) and a large pond (right) to a gate on the left giving onto a stony track up to **Yarrow Reservoir**. Follow the track to a road at a gate.

5 Turn left, downhill, and follow the road left and across the reservoir road, passing **The Yew Tree Inn**. Go down a dip

and up the long, steady ascent of **Nickelton Brow** to a T-junction. Go left into New Road.

6 Turn left again at **Horrobin Lane**. Go down and cross between reservoirs, and then take the first turning on the right rising through a small car park onto a **woodland track**. As this forks, keep ahead (right), and soon return to the start.

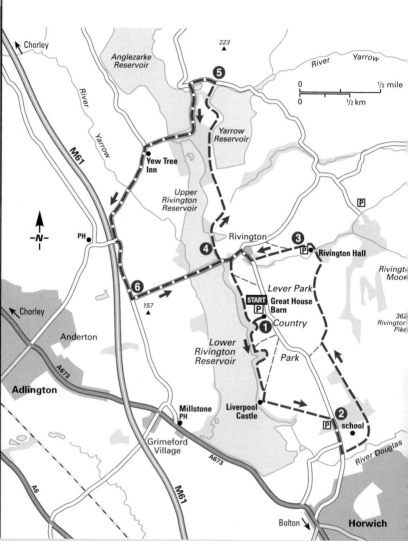

Rivington LANCASHIRE

The Millstone

Occupying a glorious position overlooking Rivington Reservoir, the old Millstone pub has been stylishly converted into a contemporary bar-restaurant serving modern European food. Although, not really a 'pub' in the true sense of the word, you will find the atmosphere friendly and informal and the lunchtime menu light and good value. In addition, there's a splendid garden for summer eating and drinking, and it is a popular meeting place among local walking and cycling groups. It has a relaxing interior with wooden floors and wall panelling and a vibrant Mediterranean-style décor.

Food

Food is freshly prepared and takes in an imaginative range of eight pasta dishes among the lunchtime selection. Other dishes may include mustard and honey-glazed ham, roast lamb shank, and slow-roasted duck leg with sea salt and rosemary.

about the pub

The Millstone
Bolton Road, Anderton
Chorley, Lancashire PR6 9HJ
Tel: 01257 480205
www.sanrocco.co.uk

DIRECTIONS: on the A673, 1 mile (1.6km) north west of Horwich. Turn right from the car park to the A673 at Horwich and turn right for the pub

PARKING: 80

OPEN: all day Saturday & Sunday; closed Monday except Bank Holidays

FOOD: daily; all day Sunday

BREWERY/COMPANY: Free House

REAL ALE: none served

Family facilities

Children are very welcome here and smaller portions of all main meals are available.

Alternative refreshment stops

Picnic sites on the ride, the Yew Tree Inn and restaurants in Horwich and Anderton.

☛ Where to go from here

North of Chorley stands the Hoghton Tower, a fortified 16th-century house with a fascinating history. It was here in 1617 that the sirloin steak came into being, when King James I famously knighted a loin of beef. Cedar Farm Galleries at Mawdesley, 6 miles (9.7km) east of Chorley, offers contemporary crafts, unique shops, a café, farm animals and a funky playground (www.lancashiretourism.com).

Haigh Country Park

Visit the seat of the Earls of Balcarres and discover the woodlands of Haigh.

Haigh Hall

You can't go in, but Haigh Hall was previously the home of the Earl of Crawford and Balcarres, and is a listed building dating back to 1850. The nearby stable buildings have been converted to a small museum, café and gift shop, with a children's play area near by. There's also a miniature railway, which operates during the summer months. Keep an eye open along the canal for birdlife, especially kingfishers which are more common here than might be imagined. Just on the edge of the estate, along Copperas Lane, is a small pond. It was formerly used for curling, and is known as the 'Curling Pond'. Kingfishers love the overhanging branches from which to feed.

the ride

1 Leave the car park and turn left (beware speed ramps), and follow a hedgerowed lane that soon starts to descend to a junction with the B5239. This B-road is well used, but there is a wide **footpath** on the right-hand side, which can be used, if necessary,

to walk to the Leeds–Liverpool Canal. Follow the road to **traffic lights** controlling the narrow bridge spanning the canal.

2 Turn left onto the canal tow path at the **Crawford Arms** pub, and follow the tow path to an **iron trellis bridge** (No. 60) – take care on the small humpback bridge just before it. Here leave the tow path, and carry bikes up a few steps to meet the main **estate road** through Haigh.

3 Turn right, and after about 100 yards (91m), turn right again on a broad drive leading out to a gate, near a cottage, at the top of **Hall Lane**. Ride down the lane (rough in places, but motorable, and a popular way into the woodlands of Haigh). Approaching the River Douglas, Hall Lane takes a wide sweep down to the **bridge** spanning the river, from which it climbs to meet the A49, at a T-junction.

4 Go left, and, if necessary, walk the 200 yards (182m) to the main Wigan entrance to **Haigh Country Park**, passing through ornate iron gates. Follow the broad, descending track ahead, which soon crosses the Douglas. Bear right, following the main track as it curves around and begins the long, steady climb back up to the **Leeds–Liverpool Canal**, and then on to the straight drive leading directly to the front of **Haigh Hall**.

5 Keep to the right of the Hall, and go up the road behind it. **The Stables Centre**, café and shop, are on the right. The car park is directly ahead, just beyond the golf shop. Turn left into the car park to complete the ride.

The golf course at Haigh Country Park

1h00 — **6 MILES** — **9.7 KM** — **LEVEL 2**

MAP: OS Explorer 276 Bolton, Wigan and Warrington

START/FINISH: Haigh Country Park; grid ref: SD 596088

TRAILS/TRACKS: canal tow path, surfaced estate or traffic roads. Stretch of 220yds (200m) on a wide town road, which can be walked. There are no cycle trails within Haigh Country Park; cyclists are asked to use the roads and trails with care for other users

LANDSCAPE: woodland, farmland and canal tow path

PUBLIC TOILETS: Stables Centre, near start

TOURIST INFORMATION: Wigan Pier, tel 01942 825677

CYCLE HIRE: none locally

THE PUB: Balcarres Arms, Haigh

🚫 One long, steady climb. Beware speed ramps on estate roads and care to be taken alongside the canal

Getting to the start

Haigh Country Park is within easy reach of both the M6 (Junction 27) and the M61 (Junction 6). From the M6, take the A49 towards Standish, then the B5239 to Haigh. Look out for the B5239 and Aspull, then Haigh, when leaving the M61. In Haigh, turn down Copperas Lane, near the Balcarres Arms, to reach the car park.

Why do this cycle ride?

Haigh Country Park has many attractions for children and the woodlands have great appeal plus almost 100 species of birds during the year. The Leeds to Liverpool Canal through the park provides an excellent opportunity to explore.

Researched and written by: Terry Marsh

CYCLE

Haigh Country Park

LANCASHIRE

The sweeping driveway and symmetrical façade of Haigh Hall

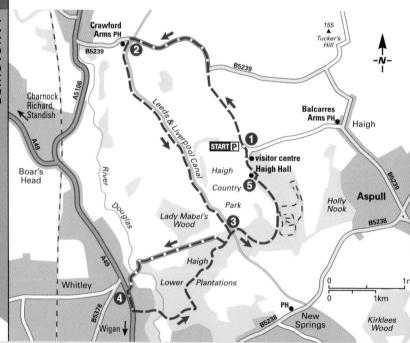

Balcarres Arms

Named after the Earl of Balcarres, who lived at nearby Haigh Hall, this is an unpretentious pub of some antiquity tucked away in historic Haigh, close to Haigh Country Park. Very much a locals' haunt, it is simply furnished and decorated and comprises a main bar and a cosy snug bar, and serves unfussy, home-cooked pub food.

Food
Expect sandwiches and light lunchtime snacks alongside home-made minted lamb casserole, Cock 'n' Bull (chicken and beef in a creamy pepper sauce), beef Madras and a range of vegetarian meals like vegetable lasagne and aubergine moussaka.

about the pub

Balcarres Arms
1 Copperas Lane, Haigh
Wigan, Lancashire WN2 1PA
Tel: 01942 833377

DIRECTIONS: beside the Country Park access road in Haigh village, 0.5 mile (800m) from the start point of the ride	
PARKING: 50	
OPEN: daily; all day	
FOOD: daily; all day Sunday, no food Tuesday evening	
BREWERY/COMPANY: Burtonwood	
REAL ALE: none served	

Family facilities
Children are allowed inside and there's a standard children's menu for younger family members. Garden with picnic benches for summer alfresco drinking.

Alternative refreshment stops
The Stables café at the end of the route.

☛ Where to go from here
Head for Wigan Pier for a journey never to be forgotten. Part museum, part theatre, it is a mixture of entertainment and education. Step back in time at 'The Way We Were' heritage centre, visit Trencherfield Mill and the Machinery Hall, and then visit the Opie's Museum of Memories. There are also walks, talks, boat trips, events and much more.

Around Comberbach

An exploration of rural
landscapes on quiet
country lanes.

Willowherb

Stag heads are old trees, usually oak, with
dead outer branches that resemble antlers.
They are a common feature of the British
countryside. Keep an eye open, too, for
stands of great willowherb: this relative
of the more common rosebay willowherb
flourishes well along the country lanes
of Cheshire and goes by a number of
interesting names – cherry pie, apple
pie and codlins-and-cream – across the
country. 'Codlins' is an old, local name
for cooking apples, and it is said that the
flower and leaves of the great willowherb,
when crushed, smell like apples, though
it is a fragrance few can detect. The
rosebay willowherb many regard as an
invasive plant, but its ability to thrive on

impoverished ground, is why it was the
first plant to colonise the sites in London
devastated during World War Two. During
Victorian times, however, it was often
grown in gardens, and was by no means
as widespread as it has now become.

the ride

1 Ride out from the car park onto **Marbury
Lane**, and at the main road, turn right.
Take care on emerging at what is an
awkward bend. Ride up to the village of
Comberbach (pavement on the right,
if needed). In the village turn left onto
Senna Lane. Go past the post office
and village stores (signed for Frandley).
Beyond the last houses, the route runs
along hedged lanes that lead to a junction.
Bear right for Whitley, and keep going to
the village of **Frandley**, there bearing left,
and going forward into **Well Lane** (for
Higher Whitley).

MAP: OS Explorer 267 Northwich and Delamere Forest

START/FINISH: Marbury Country Park (pay); grid ref: SJ 653764

TRAILS/TRACKS: on roads throughout, mostly narrow, hedged country lanes used mainly by farm vehicles

LANDSCAPE: largely agricultural, with arable fields, hedgerows, trees and copses

PUBLIC TOILETS: none on route

TOURIST INFORMATION: Chester, tel 01244 402111

CYCLE HIRE: none locally

THE PUB: The Spinner & Bergamot Inn, Comberbach

🛈 The start is along a moderately busy road, but with a pavement on one side, very short spell (33 yards/30m) on an A-road, with the option of walking on the footpath

Getting to the start

Comberbach lies 2.5 miles (4km) north west from Northwich, and Marbury Country Park between the two. The start is best reached from Northwich along the A533 to Anderton, and from the A559 along minor roads to Comberbach. The entrance to the country park is on a bend with poor visibility.

Why do this cycle ride?

The ride provides a splendid exploration of the Cheshire countryside, making use of hedged country lanes that network a wide spread of lush arable fields and isolated pockets of woodland that form part of the wider Mersey Forest. It also provides an end-of-ride opportunity to visit the Anderton Boat Lift, a unique feature along the canal ways of Britain.

Researched and written by: Terry Marsh

2 Continue to a T-junction at the end of Well Lane, and turn right. Shortly, at the end of **Old Mill Lane**, at another T-junction, turn left into **Lake Lane**. The road immediately bends right. At the next T-junction, turn right in **Bentley's Farm Lane** (signed for Lower Stretton), and continue to reach the A559 at a crossroads near a pub.

3 Turn left along the A-road (dismount if necessary and use the footpath on the left) for a few yards, and take the turning into **School Lane**, near the telephone box. Follow School Lane until you can turn left into **Booths Lane**, which, at a junction, joins Dark Lane. Keep left into **Dark Lane** and follow this into the village of Higher Whitley, which has an attractive duck-patrolled pond at its centre. Pass the pond, bearing left for Antrobus and Arley, and later turning right into **Normans Lane**. At the next junction, go right into **Old Mill Lane**.

Left: Farmland near Comberbach village
Top: Quiet country lane at Comberbach

18

🚲 CYCLE

Comberbach CHESHIRE

4 At the end of the lane, turn left into **Goosebrook Lane**, which soon climbs gently before levelling and descending gently. At the far end of the lane, at a Y-junction, turn right into **Hall Lane**, and keep on to the next T-junction, there going left for Comberbach.

5 At the next junction turn right into **Hough Lane** (signed for Barnton),

and follow the lane, climbing gently. At the next junction, branch left, still in Hough Lane, finally leaving Hough Lane at the next junction, by going forward onto **Cogshall Lane**. Follow the lane to a T-junction with a main road. Turn left and soon go steeply downhill (pavement on the right), through a dip and up the other side to the turning into the **Marbury Country Park**.

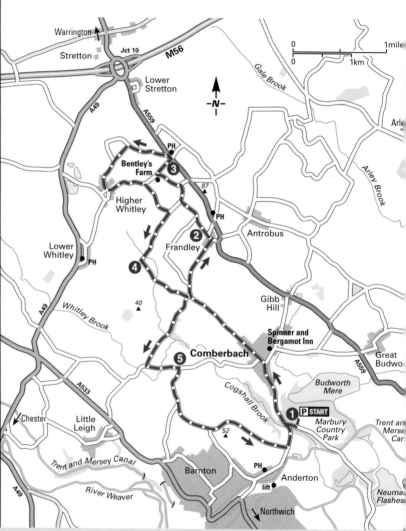

The Spinner & Bergamot Inn

Formerly called the Spinner, and built by local landed gentry, allegedly for 'private rendezvous' with mistresses, today the pub crams simple charm into its warren of small rooms decorated with Toby jugs and horse brasses. Crackling log fires add warmth and cheery welcome on cold winter days. Outside, summer seating is available on a terrace, which overlooks a Crown bowling green.

Food
Food is freshly prepared using local produce, including locally made ice creams and bread from the village baker. Typically, the menu may offer Bury black pudding for starters followed by medley of butcher's sausages with mash and onion gravy, and sausage, bacon and blue cheese casserole.

Family facilities
Children are welcome in the bars. There's no children's menu but smaller portions of many of the main dishes are available.

Alternative refreshment stops
Picnic tables throughout Marbury Country Park plus a barbecue site.

☛ Where to go from here
Take a trip to remember on the world's first boat lift. Experience the fully restored and re-opened Anderton Boat lift and watch the lift operators at work (www.andertonboatlift.co.uk). Children aged between 2 and 13 will love Gullivers World Theme Park at Warrington

about the pub

The Spinner & Bergamot Inn
Warrington Road, Comberbach
Northwich, Cheshire CW9 6AY
Tel: 01606 891307

DIRECTIONS: at the junction with Budworth Lane in the centre of Comberbach, a mile (1.6km) from Marbury Country Park	
PARKING: 110	
OPEN: daily; all day	
FOOD: daily; all day Wednesday to Sunday	
BREWERY/COMPANY: free house	
REAL ALE: Greene King IPA & Old Speckled Hen, Marston's Pedigree	

(www.gulliversfun.co.uk/warrington.htm). Don't miss Walton Hall Gardens (www.warrington.gov.uk/entertainment /parks/walton.htm).

From Wrenbury to Marbury

Visit ancient villages and explore rural Cheshire at its best.

Wrenbury Church

The church of St Margaret's in Wrenbury is dedicated to St Margaret of Antioch, a popular figure in the Middle Ages, a third-century martyr and the patron saint of expectant mothers. Today's church dates from around 1500, built from fine red Cheshire sandstone brought from the nearby Bickerton Hills. There was a chapel on this site, dating from the twelfth century. Just inside the south door is a single pew, which used to be occupied by a colourful character in village life. He was the Dog Whipper, a title which changed into a more dignified 'Beadle' in 1826. His duties were not necessarily to keep dogs out of the church – the Squire's dog, for example, was always welcome – but to evict dogs that interrupted the service. His duties also included prodding any worshippers who may have nodded off during the long sermons.

The church is particularly well-endowed with grotesque gargoyles, which took the water off the tower and aisle roofs, and other carvings may also be found, many with amusing faces, depicting the sense of humour, and sometimes sense of mischief, of medieval masons.

A canal boat passing through the bridge at Wrenbury

the ride

1 Start from the **village green** and ride left into Cholmondeley Road, gently downhill to reach and cross the **Shropshire Union Canal**. Immediately over the canal, go left alongside it. The road soon moves away from the canal, and undulates gently through lush farmland. At a side-road junction, bear left for **Norbury** following the main road, and at the next junction, turn left into **Gauntons Bank**, heading for Marbury. The road climbs gently, and then steeply for a while, to meet **School Lane**.

2 Turn left onto a descending narrow lane flanked by hedgerows, which runs on to re-cross the Shropshire Union Canal, and continues into the village of Marbury. At the end of **School Lane**, at a junction with **Wirswall Road**, turn right, soon descending around a bend.

3 Take the next turning on the left (signed for **Wirswall**), the road once again undulating. Keep following the narrow main road, ignoring joining lanes right and left, and gradually the road begins to climb into Wirswall, a long climb up towards a **radio mast**. Go past **Wood Farm** and **Wicksted Hall**, still climbing, and continue through a section with very high hedgerows. Eventually, you reach a long descent, steep in places, which leads down to a **T-junction**, not far from the centre of Whitchurch (though this is not obvious).

4 Turn left, climbing once more on a broad road to pass a small **industrial estate** before levelling and running on between mainly hawthorn hedgerows, with the road starting to narrow and descend.

The parish church in Wrenbury

2h30 – **12 MILES** – **19 KM** – **LEVEL 2**

CYCLE

MAP: OS Explorer 257 Crewe and Nantwich

START/FINISH: roadside parking beside Wrenbury village green; grid ref: SJ 595477

TRAILS/TRACKS: entirely on roads and country lanes, potholed in places

LANDSCAPE: rural Cheshire farmland

PUBLIC TOILETS: none on route

TOURIST INFORMATION: Nantwich, tel 01270 610983

CYCLE HIRE: none locally

THE PUB: The Dusty Miller, Wrenbury

🅘 Numerous undulations and some long steady ascents and descents

Getting to the start

Wrenbury is a small village between Nantwich and Whitchurch. It is most easily reached from the A49, leaving it at Cholmondeley for minor roads to Chorley and Wrenbury. On reaching Wrenbury, continue over the canal bridge and keep forward to the village green.

Why do this cycle ride?

The villages of Wrenbury and Marbury which feature in this ride, are splendidly typical of ancient, rural Cheshire, both having pedigrees extending back to Norman times. The ride travels numerous country lanes, many flanked by neatly managed hedgerows of some antiquity.

Researched and written by: Terry Marsh

Wrenbury CHESHIRE

At a road junction, bear right for **Wrenbury**, along a narrow, undulating road, to cross a railway bridge. At the next junction, bear left into **Ossmere Lane,** onto a long gentle climb past a sizeable stand of Scots pine on the right, and then climbing past a small broad-leaved woodland to another junction. Bear right for Wrenbury with distant views now appearing on the left of the **Peckforton Hills**. Follow the road (**Hollyhurst Road**), out to a T-junction just beyond a railway bridge.

Turn right into Wrenbury Road. At **Pinsley Green**, keep forward into New Road, a long straight road descending gently and flanked by low hedgerows and oak trees. This leads directly back to the **village green** in Wrenbury.

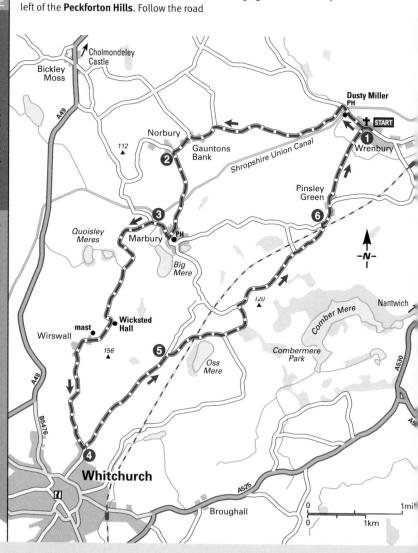

The Dusty Miller

A black-and-white lift bridge, designed by Thomas Telford, completes the picture-postcard setting for this beautifully converted 16th-century mill beside the Shropshire Union Canal. The current landlord is the great-grandson of Arthur Summer, who ran the mill up until World War Two. There's a light and airy interior with high-arched windows facing the canal, a mixture of furnishings – rustic tables, banquette seating, church pews – and hunting prints on terracotta walls. Super summer alfresco seating on a raised gravel terrace beside the River Weaver and canal.

Food

The menu, which increasingly uses ingredients sourced from the north west, might offer smoked fresh haddock and prawns baked in a Staffordshire oatcake, slow-roasted duck breast with Cumberland sauce and garlic mash, jugged beef, home-made soups and a good selection of sandwiches.

Family facilities

Children of all ages are allowed in the pub. Youngsters have their own menu and older children can order small portions from the main menu. There are also high chairs.

Alternative refreshment stops

Restaurants and pubs in Whitchurch near Point 4 on the route and a pub at Marbury.

☛ Where to go from here

Hack Green Secret Nuclear Bunker, for 50 years Cheshire's nuclear headquarters, was a secret known only to Civil Service emergency planners. Now preserved, tou can explore the blast-proof HQ, war rooms, TV studios and see film footage of the day (www.hackgreen.co.uk). The bunker is south of Nantwich, just off the A530.

about the pub

The Dusty Miller
Cholmondeley Road,
Wrenbury
Nantwich, Cheshire CW5 8HG
Tel: 01270 780537
www.dustymiller-wrenbury.com

DIRECTIONS: by the canal (on the route), 500 yds (460m) from the village and start point of the ride	
PARKING: 50	
OPEN: daily; all day	
FOOD: daily; no food Mondays in winter	
BREWERY/COMPANY: Robinsons Brewery	
REAL ALE: Robinsons Best, Old Stockport Bitter, Hatters Mild, Frederics Bitter, XB & Old Tom	

Hurst Green   LANCASHIRE

Hurst Green and the Three Rivers

Did these rivers, fields and woods inspire Tolkien's creation of The Shire?

Tolkien connection

J R R Tolkien, author of *The Lord of the Rings*, knew this area well and he spent long periods here while writing the trilogy. In the hobbits' Shire there's a River Shirebourn and the Shireburn family once owned Stonyhurst. But does that mean that Hurst Green is Hobbiton? A locally available leaflet gives more detail.

Just after reaching the Ribble, you pass an aqueduct, then an easy 0.75 mile (1.2km) brings you to Jumbles Rock, outcrops of limestone, which form natural weirs and a ford. The isolated Boat House was a ferryman's home. In the fields near by are two obvious mounds. The lower one was excavated in 1894 and dated to around 1250. The larger, though known to be artificial, has yet to be properly examined. As the Ribble swings round, the River

Calder enters opposite, close to 17th-century Hacking Hall. Less than 0.75 mile (1.2km) further on is the confluence of the Ribble and the Hodder, which you follow briefly, leaving it near Winckley Hall. You return to the river at Low Hodder Bridge.

You follow the Hodder for almost another mile (1.6km) before climbing steeply away to Woodfields. Tolkien stayed in one of these houses. The track passes St Mary's Hall and then reaches Hall Barn Farm. Near by, on the edge of Stoneyhurst's precincts is a small observatory, one of a network.

the walk

1 Walk down the road to the centre of Hurst Green village. Cross the main road and go down left of the **Shireburn Arms** to a stile below the main car park. Go down the edge of a field, when possible move to the right of a small **stream** and follow it to some duckboards and a footbridge. After a slight rise, **wooden steps** wind down to another footbridge just before the **River Ribble**.

A fisherman standing in the waters of the Ribble

| 2h30 | 6.5 MILES | 10.4 KM | LEVEL 1 2 3 |

Bear left just above the river.

2 Skirt the aqueduct and return to the river bank. A gravel track swings right past **Jumbles**. Stay on the track towards the **Boat House,** and there bear right to the river bank.

3 After rounding the big bend, go up slightly to a **track**. Follow this for about 0.5 mile (800m). Opposite the confluence of the Ribble and the Hodder, keep forward through a **gate**.

4 Continue along the track to **Winckley Hall Farm**. There go left to the houses, right between barns then left past a pond and out into a lane. This climbs steadily, then levels out, swinging left past **Winckley Hall**. Go through a kissing gate on the right and across the field to another. Keep straight on across a large field, just left of a wood, then down past a **pond** and across to a road.

5 Turn right down a pavement to the river. Immediately before the **bridge**, turn left along a track. Follow the river round, climb up past **Hodder Place** then descend again to a bridge over a stream.

6 Go left along a track, cross a footbridge then climb a long flight of wooden steps. Follow the top edge of a **plantation** then cross a stile into a field. Keep to its edge and at the end cross a stile into a stony track. Keep left, to pass **Woodfields** and out to the road. Go down the track by

A run-down barn with vegetation starting to encroach upon it, Ribbleside

MAP: OS Explorer 287 West Pennine Moors
START/FINISH: car park at Hurst Green village hall or on roadside adjacent; grid ref: SD 684382
PATHS: grassy riverside paths, woodland and farm tracks, 12 stiles
LANDSCAPE: pastoral scenery, scattered woodlands, backdrop of moors
PUBLIC TOILETS: centre of Hurst Green
TOURIST INFORMATION: Clitheroe, tel 01200 425566
THE PUB: The Shireburn Arms, Hurst Green

Getting to the start

Hurst Green is a quiet but popular village north of the River Ribble, and about 5 miles (8km) south west of Clitheroe on the B6243 to Longridge. Parking at the village hall.

Researched and written by:
Terry Marsh, Jon Sparks

the post-box to **Hall Barn Farm** and along the right side of the buildings.

7 Turn right on a tarmac track for 200yds (183m). Go left through a gate by the end of a wall and along the left-hand side of a narrow field. Follow a grassy path bearing right to a path alongside a wood, then up to a kissing gate. Follow the field edge to another kissing gate. At the top of the final field, through a gate, a narrow path leads to a short lane. At its end turn left back to the start.

what to look for

One plant to look out for, especially along the riversides, is butterbur. This is another name that will ring bells with Tolkien devotees; there's an innkeeper in The Lord of the Rings called Barliman Butterbur. The flower spikes, which appear in early spring, look superficially like dull pinkish hyacinths, but the individual flowers are daisy-like. Later in the year huge leaves develop, which were traditionally used to wrap butter.

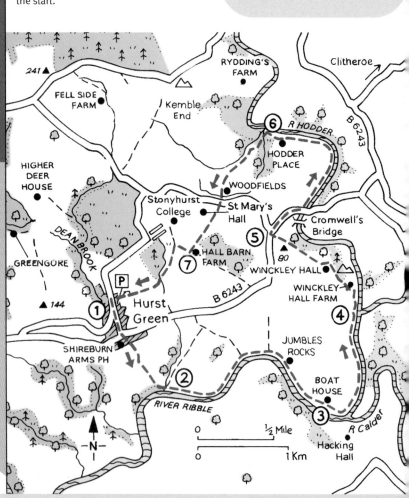

The Shireburn Arms

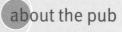

In the absence of a Green Dragon or Prancing Pony, the Shireburn Arms has the most Tolkeinesque name, and it's a very comfortable place, if a little bit upmarket for hobbits – you'll probably want to change out of muddy boots first. A focal point of the village since it was built in the 17th-century, this civilised small hotel enjoys an idyllic setting with fine views over the Ribble Valley to the Pennines. The lovely beamed lounge bar serves locally brewed Bowland ales on handpump, and there's a smart restaurant as well as a good range of bar food. The neat rear terrace and gardens are perfect for peaceful post-walk refreshment on warm sunny days.

Food
From the bar menu, order sandwiches, ham and eggs, shepherd's pie, vegetable lasagne, liver and onions, pork Stroganoff or steak and kidney pudding.

Family facilities
Like many good hotels, children are warmly welcomed here and you'll find a children's menu, high chairs, toys to keep little ones amused, a play area in the garden and three family bedrooms.

Alternative refreshment stops
The Bayley Arms in Hurst Green and there's a tea room at Stonyhurst College (if visiting).

☞ Where to go from here
Ribchester Roman Museum (www.ribchestermuseum.org) contains many impressive artefacts excavated from the area including urns, coins, jewellery and a ceremonial helmet. Visit the ruins

about the pub

The Shireburn Arms
Whalley Road, Hurst Green
Clitheroe, Lancashire BB7 9QJ
Tel: 01254 826518
www.shireburnarms.fsnet.co.uk

DIRECTIONS: see Getting to the Start; inn beside the B6243 in the village centre

PARKING: 120

OPEN: daily; all day

FOOD: daily; all day Sunday

BREWERY/COMPANY: free house

REAL ALE: Bowland Brewery beers

DOGS: allowed in the bar

ROOMS: 18 en suite

of 14th-century Whalley Abbey (south of Clitheroe), set in the delightful gardens of a retreat and conference centre, or explore Clitheroe Castle's 12th-century Norman keep and fascinating museum, which houses exhibits relating to the history and geology of the local area (www.ribblevalley.gov.uk).

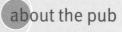

20

WALK

Hurst Green

LANCASHIRE

Darwen Tower and moors

Darwen Moors

LANCASHIRE

A simple walk, if moderately steep in parts, to a great physical and historical landmark on the moors.

Darwen Moors

The opening stages of the walk are a pleasant preamble, through the woods around Upper Roddlesworth Reservoir and over a shoulder by some old tracks to Earnsdale Reservoir. Here you are just above Sunnyhurst Wood, Darwen's main park, which provides a direct link from the town on to the moors. Above the reservoirs you climb in stages. After the old quarry you begin the final, longest stage, on a corner of the moors overlooking the town. The dominant feature is India Mill dating from the 1860s. The chimney is 302ft (92m) high and its style is not Indian but Italianate. The

mill closed in 1991 but now houses new light industry and office space.

Construction of Darwen Tower began in 1897, the year after achievement of the right to roam on the moor. There are 65 wide stone steps, and 16 iron ones leading to the small glasshouse on the top. The tower fell into some decay but has been restored, with funds from a public appeal.

Naturally the view is extensive, especially in the northern half. Some of it has changed totally since the tower was built; the new industrial areas alongside the M65 above Blackburn are the most obvious example. But the skylines of Bowland and Pendle are the same. The descent takes you past some old mine workings and a waterworks channel. Just before the end, the row of houses (Hollinshead Terrace) was built as workers' accommodation for a nearby mill that no longer exists.

square-shaped Sunnyhurst Hey Reservoir seen from Darwen Tower

2h00 — **4 MILES** **6.4 KM** **LEVEL 123**

The walk

1. From the car park cross a bus turning area and then the road. Go through some gates and reach a footpath sign in 30yds (27m). Go right, following the sign for **'Woods and Water Trail'**. The path descends steadily to a cross-path. Turn right here on a broad path – still the 'Woods and Water Trail' – then after 200yds (183m) go right at a fork on a gently rising path. Gradually curve to the right and climb a little more steeply, with open fields on the left, out to the road. Go left for 200yds (183m).

2. Go right up a walled track, part of the **Witton Weavers' Way**. Go straight on at crossroads then descend steeply, with a section of old paving, towards **Earnsdale Reservoir**. Cross the dam and swing left at its end then follow the lane up right until it swings left once more, over a cattle grid. Go straight up the steep grass slope on the right to meet a track.

3. Go left on the track then, just after a **house**, bear right up a concrete track. As the track bends right, go through a gap in the aluminium barrier and bear left on a level path towards an **old quarry**. As this is reached, go up right on a stony track. Above a gate, keep left where it forks. A gate on the left, flanked by fine flagstones, gives a good view of the town of Darwen, dominated by the **India Mill chimney**. Continue up the main track for another 100yds (91m). As the gradient eases and

Darwen Tower was started in 1897, a year after the hard-won right to roam on the moor

MAP: OS Explorer 287 West Pennine Moors

START/FINISH: car park near Royal Arms; grid ref: SD 665215

PATHS: well-defined tracks throughout, 3 stiles

LANDSCAPE: reservoir and wooded surroundings, farmland, open moors

PUBLIC TOILETS: at car park

TOURIST INFORMATION: Blackburn, tel 01254 53277

THE PUB: Royal Arms, Tockholes

⚠ Some fairly steep sections

Getting to the start

Tockholes lies within the West Pennine Moors, only 2 miles (3.2km) west of Darwen, but is most easily accessible from the A666 and A6062 south of Blackburn to the north. Car park and toilets just south of the Royal Arms.

Researched and written by:
Terry Marsh, Jon Sparks

the tower comes into view bear right, past a **marker stone** on which there's a likeness of the tower, and straight up to the real thing.

4 From the tower bear left past the **trig point** and along a broad path above the steeper slope that falls to **Sunnyhurst Hey Reservoir**. The path swings left past a bench. Go over the second stile on the right overlooking the valley of **Stepback Brook** and down a path. Don't cross the next stile but go down left, to a stile beside a gate. Go left on a track.

5 The track swings right and up through a wood. As it levels out pass to the

right of a pair of gates and continue down towards a row of **houses**. A lane just left o these leads to the road. Go back past the bus turning area to the car park.

what to look for

You can look, with care, for old coal-mine shafts on the moor, in the area where you begin to descend. Usually there's little left to see but a conical pit, with scattered spoil heaps near by forming good markers, but one or two still have open shafts. The deepest of the shafts went down around 200ft (61m).

Royal Arms

Set high on the moors above Blackburn, the Royal Arms has an old-fashioned feel inside, with its several small and unpretentious rooms featuring open log fires, cracking ales from Isle of Man micro-breweries, and a traditional decor, though in a welcome modern development one room is no smoking. Bustling and very friendly, it is particularly popular with walkers – there's a nature trail opposite – and the big garden is a real a sun trap with fine views of Darwen Tower.

Food
The menu is also fairly traditional but still provides a reasonable choice of good home cooked meals. It constantly changes with the seasons, often listing summer fish and lobster specials and local game in winter. Good bar snacks.

Family facilities
Children are allowed inside the pub but there are no special facilities, although the garden does have a play area to keep them amused on fine days.

Alternative refreshment stops
There's nothing along the route, but the nearby Victoria Hotel in Tockholes is also a popular destination for walkers.

☛ Where to go from here
Tockholes village, which lies below the main road, is best explored on foot as its streets are narrow in places. There are several fine 17th-century houses and the village school, dating from 1854, has an external pulpit which allowed open-air preaching. West of Blackburn is Samlesbury Hall, a well restored half-timbered manor house, built during the 14th and 15th centuries, and set in 2 hectares (5 acres) of beautiful grounds (www.samlesburyhall.co.uk). South of Darwen you will find Turton Tower, an historic house incorporating a 15th-century tower house and Elizabethan half-timbered buildings, and displaying a major collection of carved wood furniture (www.bolton.org.uk).

about the pub

Royal Arms
Tockholes Road, Tockholes
Darwen, Lancashire BB3 0PA
Tel: 01254 705373

DIRECTIONS: see Getting to the start	
PARKING: 50	
OPEN: all day; closed Monday	
FOOD: all day; no food Tuesday evening	
BREWERY/COMPANY: free house	
REAL ALE: O'Kells Bitter, Bushy's beers, guest beers	
DOGS: allowed in the bar	

Gisburn Forest

Explore Lancashire's biggest forest and discover its flora and fauna.

Gisburn Forest

Gisburn Forest is Lancashire's biggest, covering 3,000 acres (1,215ha). It was opened in 1932, around the same time as Stocks Reservoir, alongside it. The reservoir is huge, formed by damming the River Hodder and submerging the village of Stocks in the process of providing drinking water for the towns of central Lancashire. When it's full it can hold 2.6 billion gallons. Gisburn Forest and Stocks Reservoir are favoured places for birdwatchers. In springtime, keep an eye open for visiting osprey, which quite often use the reservoir for on-the-wing food supplies on their way northwards to Scotland at breeding time.

You will almost certainly spot members of the tit family, notably great, blue and coal tits, and may be lucky to see a great-spotted woodpecker. This is a good time, too, to look for orchids: Gisburn is renowned for its common spotted orchid, which flourishes in the damp conditions.

the ride

1 Set off along a narrow path from the car park, to a sharp left-hand bend, then descend, before climbing gently to pass a barrier, and reach a **broad forest trail**. Turn right, and about 100 yards (110m) later, when the track forks, keep forward. Before reaching a group of buildings (**Stephen Park**), leave the broad trail and turn right at a waymark onto a very narrow path that follows the edge of an open area, and finally heads back towards the buildings.

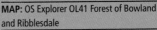

1h00 · **6 MILES** · **9.7 KM** · **LEVEL 2**

2 On reaching **Stephen Park**, turn right on a broad trail, which immediately forks. Keep left, climbing gently, and then heading downhill. Continue following the main trail as it weaves a way through the forest to a **barrier** coming up to a T-junction, where the three main forest cycle trails divide. Here turn left, pursuing the **Purple Trail**.

3 Continue to the access to **Hesbert Hall Farm**, and there branch right, passing a barrier into a short stretch of dense woodland with a clearing ahead. Now make a long descent to cross a **stream**, beyond which the track rises to a T-junction, where the Red and Green route rejoin. Turn left.

Top: Picnic tables in Gisburn Forest
Below: A view from the Gisburn Forest Trail

MAP: OS Explorer OL41 Forest of Bowland and Ribblesdale

START/FINISH: Cocklet Hill car park; grid ref: SD 746550

TRAILS/TRACKS: mainly broad forest trails, some narrow paths and stony, bumpy trails

LANDSCAPE: forest

PUBLIC TOILETS: none on route

TOURIST INFORMATION: Clitheroe, tel 01200 425566

CYCLE HIRE: Pedal Power, Waddington Road, Clitheroe, Lancashire BB7 2HJ, tel 01200 422066

THE PUB: The Hark to Bounty, Slaidburn

🛈 Maps are useless in Gisburn - follow the Purple Trail. Stony trails and overhanging vegetation

Getting to the start

Gisburn Forest is well signed across the surrounding countryside, but the start is best reached along the B6478 from Slaidburn (south west) or Long Preston (north east).

Why do this cycle ride?

Forests like Gisburn are known for mile after mile of conifers with scarcely a decent view. But at Gisburn, more and more broadleaved trees are being planted, and areas are being cleared to allow for good views. The trails in Gisburn are waymarked; this route follows the shortest, the Purple Trail. Maps can't keep up-to-date with what is happening on the ground, so waymark chasing is the best way.

Researched and written by: Terry Marsh

4 The broad trail eventually leads on, after winding through the forest, to another T-junction. Here, turn left, descending, and following a bumpy route that brings **Stocks Reservoir** into view. Eventually, just before reaching a road, turn left at a **waymark post** onto a narrow path through mixed woodland to reach the **road**, which now crosses an arm of the reservoir.

5 On the other side, leave the road by turning left up a steep and narrow path – you may have to dismount here. Follow this through **woodland**, steep in places, and finally emerge at a broad forest track at a bend. Keep left and then forward, and climb to another **barrier** giving on to a T-junction. Turn right, and 100yds (110m) later turn left, having now rejoined the outward route, which is retraced to the start.

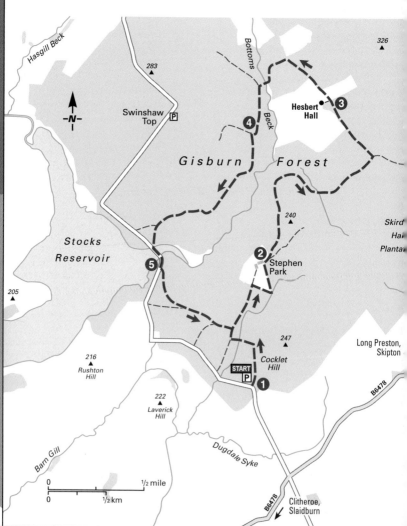

The Hark to Bounty

The setting – a beautiful village on the moors above Clitheroe – is one of the attractions of this historic stone pub. It dates from the 13th century and was known as the The Dog until 1875 when Bounty, the local squire's favourite hound, disturbed a post-inn drinking session with its loud baying. View the original first floor courtroom, for many years the main court between Lancaster and York, and still in use until 1937. It's now a function room, complete with old jury benches and a witness box. Downstairs, the atmospheric old bar has old-fashioned settles, exposed beams, a roaring log fire, plenty of brass ornaments and old pictures on the walls.

Food
Traditional favourites include home-made fish, steak and kidney pies, vegetable and cheese crumble, and grilled haddock topped with tomatoes and Lancashire cheese, supplemented by pasta and curries from the chalkboards. Snacks take in filled jacket potatoes and ploughman's lunches.

Family facilities
Children are very welcome throughout and there's a children's menu, high chairs, smaller portions and changing facilities.

Alternative refreshment stops
None on the route. Refreshments in Slaidburn and Clitheroe.

Where to go from here
Developed on the site of former 17th-century cottages, Slaidburn Heritage Centre provides a site for exhibitions and information relating to the history of this fascinating area. South of Clitheroe are the 14th-century ruins of Whalley Abbey, originally a medieval monastery, set in the grounds of a 17th-century manor house, now a retreat and conference centre. Guided tours, visitor centre and coffee shop.

about the pub

The Hark to Bounty
Slaidburn, Clitheroe
Lancashire BB7 3EP
Tel: 01200 446246
www.harktobounty.co.uk

DIRECTIONS: from Gisburn Forest return to the B6478 and turn right for 3 miles (4.8km) to reach Slaidburn. Cross the river and take the second turning right for the pub

OPEN: daily; all day

FOOD: daily; all day Sunday

BREWERY/COMPANY: free house

REAL ALE: Courage Directors, Theakston Old Peculier, guest ales

ROOMS: 9 en suite

A circuit from Barley

WALK

A grand loop around the flanks and subsidiary ridges of Pendle Hill.

Pendle Witches

Pendle is associated with witches and in 1612 seven women and two men from Pendle were hanged at Lancaster Castle.

The walk starts easily, on a well-marked and much-trodden route (part of the Pendle Way) through green fields. While this loop avoids the challenge of the steep upper slopes, it does make a fairly level, but moderately rough, traverse along their base, giving a taste of the wilder atmosphere of the high moors.

From the plantations and reservoirs of Ogden Clough you climb on to a subsidiary ridge, which gives the best views of the walk, then descend to the small village of Newchurch in Pendle. Although no one

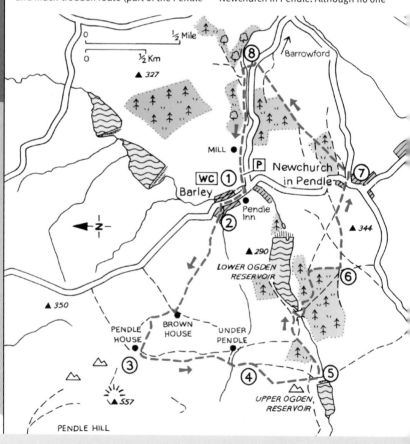

knows for sure, it is thought that Malkin Tower, where the witches met, was near by. On the tower of St Mary's Church the 'Eye of God', was supposed to protect the villagers from witchcraft, and in the churchyard there's a 'witch's grave'.

Beyond Newchurch the route follows the continuation of the ridge, looking down on Roughlee. Roughlee was the home of Alice Nutter, one of those hanged at Lancaster. Although poor, old women, especially widows, were most likely to be suspect, no one was exempt from the paranoia of the times. Anyone who kept a dog or cat, for instance, ran the risk of being accused of consorting with a 'familiar spirit'. Finally the walk follows the banks of bubbling Pendle Water, past cottages and an old mill, back to Barley.

the walk

1 From the toilets follow a path rightwards across the green then over a **footbridge**. Go right then up the street. Just past **Meadow Bank Farm** go left up a footpath alongside a stream.

2 Keep straight on up then cross another footbridge and join a lane. Follow this left, with lots of signs, to a kissing gate and a well-marked path that leads up to **Brown House** and **Pendle Hill**. Go through the yard, right on a track for 60yds (55m) then left through another kissing gate. Go up, through another kissing gate and new plantings and straight up to a gate left of **Pendle House**.

3 Go left on a path just above the wall. After another gate, climb a little, away

---

2h30 · **4.75 MILES** · **7.7 KM** · **LEVEL 1 2 3**

MAP:	OS Explorer OL21 South Pennines or OL41 Forest of Bowland & Ribblesdale
START/FINISH:	public car park in Barley village; grid ref: SD 823403
PATHS:	field paths and rough moorland, surfaced track, 10 stiles
LANDSCAPE:	wooded foothills and moorland slopes
PUBLIC TOILETS:	at car park
TOURIST INFORMATION:	Clitheroe, tel 01200 425566
THE PUB:	The Pendle Inn, Barley

🅛 This is an undulating walk which young children may find tiring

Getting to the start

Barley lies concealed in the rolling landscape on the south side of the Ribble Valley, 5 miles (8km) to the east of Clitheroe. It is best reached from the north off the A59 via Downham, and from the south by the A682 at Barrowford via Roughlee.

Researched and written by:
Terry Marsh, Jon Sparks

from the wall. The path runs an undulating course, then dips more definitely and meets the wall again. From a stile beside a gate just above **Under Pendle**, follow a fence and path to a clearer track to rejoin the wall.

4 Bear right on a path climbing alongside an obvious **groove** to a gate and stile. Ignore these, and instead go left through a gate and straight down by a wall. Cross a track and descend steeply to a gate just below **Upper Ogden Reservoir**.

5 Follow the **reservoir road** until just above Lower Ogden Reservoir. Go right over a bridge, down a few steps then right to a footbridge. Climb steps then go left and climb more steps through a **plantation**. At its end, go up right to the ridge.

6 Turn left following a **fence** then a wall to a stile. Descend by a wall, and at a signpost bear right, keeping roughly level until the rooftops of **Newchurch** appear. Aim for a **water trough**, then a stile and signpost. Descend a short path to the road.

7 Go down the road opposite, signposted for **Roughlee**. After about 100yds (91m)

what to look for

The moors of Pendle are largely grassy, less dominated by heather than those of Bowland. There's a much greater variety of plants than may initially meet the eye. Low-growing tormentil has yellow flowers like tiny Maltese crosses: you'll have to get down low to see that it's actually a member of the rose family. The unmistakable fluffy white tufts of cotton grass, also known as bog cotton, are a marker for wet ground.

cross a stile on the left-hand side and follow a **rising footpath**. Fork to the left just inside a plantation. At the far end of the **plantation** keep straight on, gradually converging with the wall on the left-hand side. Follow the wall, changing sides at the end of a plantation, and descend to a **sunken track**. Cross this and descend to the road.

8 Go down the tarmac track opposite, cross the **Pendle Water** then go left alongside it. Continue on a stonier track past some cottages and an old **mill**. Finally a short path on the right leads back to the car park.

A track bordered by a dry-stone wall near Burley

The Pendle Inn

Set at the foot of the renowned Pendle Hill in picturesque Barley village, the imposing Pendle Inn dates from the 1930s and the fine, panelled interior is original. There's an open fire, a games room, good beer from Moorhouses Brewery in nearby Burnley, including, on occasions, the amber-coloured, heady and aptly-named Pendle Witches Brew, and solid pub food, available all day. There's also a lovely summer garden and terrace outside overlooking the beck.

Food

Hearty pub fare takes in good bar snacks – sandwiches and ploughman's – and chicken Kiev, roast loin of pork, gammon steak, and silverside of beef with Yorkshire pudding.

Family facilities

Children are welcome throughout the pub. There's a children's menu for youngsters and a play area in the garden.

Alternative refreshment stops

A tea room at the Pendle Heritage Centre serves meals and snacks.

☛ Where to go from here

Pendle Heritage Centre (www.pendle.gov.uk) is 2 miles (3.2km) away, off the B6247 on the outskirts of Barrowford. In a lovingly restored 17th-century house you can find out much more about the story of the Pendle witches, and about the general history of the area. You'll also find lots of 'witch' material and souvenirs at Witches Galore in Newchurch (www.witchesgalore.co.uk). The largest mill steam engine still in working order in Barnoldswick can be seen at Bancroft Mill.

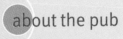

about the pub

The Pendle Inn

Barley, Burnley
Lancashire BB12 9JX
Tel: 01282 614808
www.pendleinn.freeserve.co.uk

DIRECTIONS: see Getting to the start; pub is close to the car park in the village

PARKING: 40

OPEN: daily; all day

FOOD: daily; all day

BREWERY/COMPANY: free house

REAL ALE: Moorhouses Bitter, guest beers

DOGS: allowed inside

ROOMS: 3 en suite

Pendle

LANCASHIRE

Tatton Park to Dunham Park

Link two great estates –
Tatton and Dunham – and
get the best of both worlds.

A pub and two parks

It is always fascinating to research pub names. They invariably tell a great deal about the surrounding communities and countryside. This route passes the Swan with Two Nicks (corrupted in some parts of England as the Swan with Two Necks, an improbable likelihood). The name comes from an association with the Vintners Company, founded in 1357 by importers of wine from Bordeaux. The company was incorporated by Henry VI (1422–1461) into one of the oldest of the Trade Guilds of London. Its symbol is a swan with two nicks on its beak. Then, as now, swans were the exclusive property of the Crown, but a Royal Gift was made to the Vintners, and each year the Vintners would put a nick on each side of the beak of cygnets to identify them as Vintner's swans.

The ride also links two of Britain's old estates, which offer a wealth of exploration and learning for all ages.

Tatton Park: the Mansion and Tudor Old Hall are set in 1,000 acres (405ha) of beautiful rolling parkland with lakes, tree-lined avenues and herds of deer. There are award-winning gardens, a working farm, play area, speciality shops and a superb programme of special events. There is plenty here to entertain the family, but there are extra charges for admission to the mansion, garden, farm or Tudor Old Hall.

Dunham Park: An early Georgian house built around a Tudor core, Dunham Massey was reworked in the early 20th century, to produce one of Britain's most sumptuous Edwardian interiors. It houses collections of 18th-century walnut furniture, paintings and Huguenot silver, as well as extensive servants' quarters. Here is one of the North West's great plantsman's gardens with richly planted borders and ancient trees, as well as an orangery, Victorian bark-house and well-house. The deer park contains beautiful avenues and ponds and a Tudor mill, originally used for grinding corn but refitted as a sawmill c.1860 and now restored to working order.

the ride

1 Leave the car park and ride out along the driveway to the **Rostherne Entrance** – keep an eye open for deer roaming in the park. Cross the road onto the **Cheshire Cycle Way West**, and ride on towards the village of Rostherne. Just on entering the village, turn left into **New Road**, climbing steeply for a short while, and then descending as it becomes **Cicely Mill Lane**, and leads out to a junction of two A-roads,

The award-winning gardens in the grounds of Tatton Park

CYCLE

| 2h30 | 12.5 MILES | 20 KM | LEVEL 1 2 |

MAP: OS Explorer 267 Northwich and Delamere Forest and 276 Bolton, Wigan and Warrington

START/FINISH: Tatton Park (charge for admission); grid ref: SJ 741815

TRAILS/TRACKS: Outside Tatton Park, the route is entirely on minor roads, with a major A-road crossing (at lights)

LANDSCAPE: Cheshire farmland and two major estate parks

PUBLIC TOILETS: at Tatton Hall

TOURIST INFORMATION: Knutsford, tel 01565 632611

CYCLE HIRE: none locally

THE PUB: Swan with Two Nicks, Little Bollington

🅘 Two major A-road crossings, one using traffic lights

Tatton Park

CHESHIRE

near the **Swan Hotel** at Bucklow Hill. The easiest thing to do here is dismount and cross the two roads (at traffic lights) as a pedestrian.

2 Cross into **Chapel Lane**, initially a long, straight road, leading to Hulseheath. Keep on, riding round bends, and then turn right into **Back Lane**. At a junction, go left into Thowler Lane, and at the next junction, bear right for Bollington, along **Boothbank Lane**.

3 On reaching **Booth Bank**, keep forward into **Reddy Lane** (signed for Bollington and Dunham Massey). Descend a little to pass beneath the M56 motorway, and then climbing around bends. The road eventually straightens and leads out to meet the A56, opposite a pub.

4 Cross the road with care, going left and then immediately right into **Park Lane**. Continue past the **Swan with Two Nicks** pub, to the end of the surfaced lane, where a narrow bridge crosses the **River Bollin**.

Getting to the start
The main entrance is at Rostherne. You can take the A50 from Knutsford, then branch onto the A5034 and then on to a minor road (signed for Tatton Park).

Why do this cycle ride?
The opportunity to link two of Cheshire's important estates should not be missed. The ride follows quiet lanes across farmland landscape and reaches a mill and weir on the edge of Dunham Park. Both parks have family attractions. The nearby village of Rostherne is a lovely community of brick houses with a few thatched cottages.

Researched and written by: Terry Marsh

CYCLE

5 At **Bollington Mill**, go forward, but as the road bends left leave it by branching right onto a fenced and tree-lined path into **Dunham Park**.

6 Retrace the outward route. Avoid tempting alternative routes, as **Bucklow Hill** is the safest place to cross the Chester Road (A556).

The 18th-century Dunham Massey Hall

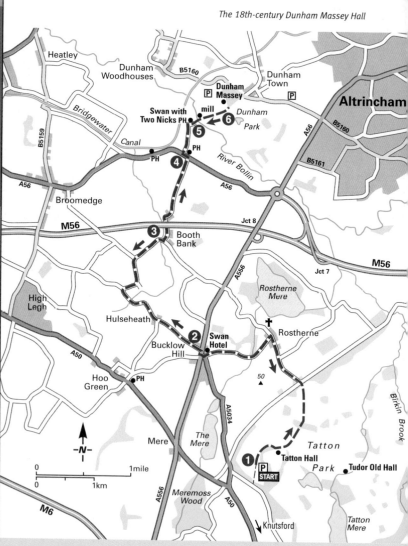

Swan with Two Nicks

Tucked away in a tiny hamlet close to Dunham Hall deer park, this distinctive, smartly refurbished pub is a real find and a super place for refreshments on this ride. Welcoming features include heavy ceiling beams, lovely antique settles, roaring winter log fires, while gleaming brass and copper artefacts and a wealth of bric-a-brac decorate the bars. There's also good seating in the patio garden, freshly prepared pub food, decent wines and three real ales on handpump.

Food

Typically, tuck into filled baguettes, various omelettes, sandwiches and salads at lunchtime, with main menu dishes including a hearty steak and ale pie, sausages and mash, grilled gammon and egg, and a range of pasta dishes.

Family facilities

A good welcome awaits families as children are allowed throughout the pub. Half portions of main meals are provided and there's a children's menu for younger family members.

Alternative refreshment stops

Stables Restaurant at Tatton Park serves hot meals, snacks and hot or cold drinks.

🖝 Where to go from here

Take a closer look at Tatton Park, one of England's most complete historic estates (www.nationaltrust.org.uk), or visit nearby Tabley House, west of Knutsford, (www.tableyhouse.co.uk), the finest Palladian house in the North West, which holds the first great collection of English pictures ever made, and furniture by

about the pub

Swan with Two Nicks

Little Bollington, Altrincham
Cheshire WA14 4TJ
Tel: 0161 928 2914

DIRECTIONS: Little Bollington is signposted off the A56 between Lymm and the M56. The pub is in the village centre at the halfway point of the ride

PARKING: 80

OPEN: daily; all day

FOOD: daily; all day Sunday

BREWERY/COMPANY: free house

REAL ALE: Timothy Taylor Landlord, Greene King Old Speckled Hen, Swan with Two Nicks Bitter

Chippendale, Gillow and Bullock. Further afield is Jodrell Bank Visitor Centre (www.jb.man.ac.uk), where a pathway leads you 180 degrees around the massive Lovell radio telescope as it surveys the Universe. There's also an arboretum, and a 3-D theatre explores the solar system.

Around Alderley Edge

Layers of history and legend surrounding this famous Cheshire landmark make this short walk a rich mixture.

Alderley Edge

There's a lot to take in at Alderley Edge, on the ground, under the ground and even – many believe – in other dimensions entirely.

As long as 4,000 years ago, there was mining activity here, which went on through Roman times and reached its greatest intensity in the 19th century. Copper and lead were the main products. Alderley Edge is as rich in legend as it is in minerals. In

fact it is probably true that it is rich in legend because of its long history of exploitation. Old shafts and levels or overgrown heaps of spoil can mystify later generations and inspire speculation. Also, working underground, especially in the fickle light of tallow candles or primitive lamps, seems to stimulate the imagination.

The most famous legend of the area is alluded to in the names of the Wizard Inn and Wizard's Well, both passed on this walk. Hidden somewhere on the Edge is a cave, guarded by a wizard, in which an army of men and horses sleeps, ready to emerge and save the country when the need is dire. No one has found this cave

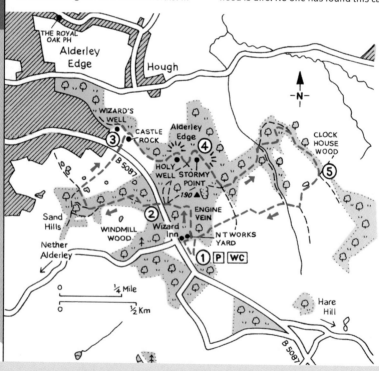

(though it must be a big one) but you can see the wizard, or at least an effigy, carved in the rocks above the Wizard's Well.

The walk itself is largely through woodland. In fact the wooded aspect of Alderley Edge is relatively recent. The demand for fuel, building timber and pit props, ensured that the area was cleared of its trees from the Bronze Age onwards. The local landowner, Lord Stanley, began extensive plantings in the mid-18th century, managed today by the National Trust.

Although the Edge is elevated above the surrounding countryside, its trees obstruct distant views. From the crest of Castle Rock there is a broad window to the north, towards Manchester with the hills of Lancashire beyond, while at Stormy Point the view opens to the east, towards the Peak District. There are exceptions to the woodland rule. Behind Sand Hills, in the earlier part of the walk, there are damp areas with many orchids, and pools fringed by yellow iris and reed mace (the tall club-headed reed often wrongly called the bulrush). Nearing the end, there's some open farmland.

the walk

1 From the large **National Trust car park**, just off the B5087, walk towards the tea room and information room. Go right on a wide track past the National Trust **works yard**, then left. Cross an open area past **Engine Vein**. At a crossroads of paths turn left and come out by **Beacon Lodge**.

2 Go straight across the road into **Windmill Wood**. Follow a gently descending track to a clearing, bear left and continue descending. At a fork, branch

1h30 — **3 MILES** — **4.8 KM** — **LEVEL 1 2 3**

MAP: OS Explorer 268 Wilmslow, Macclesfield & Congleton

START/FINISH: Large National Trust car park off B5087; grid ref: SJ 860772

PATHS: woodland tracks and paths, some field paths, 9 stiles

LANDSCAPE: woodland, scattered sandstone crags, some farmland

PUBLIC TOILETS: at car park

TOURIST INFORMATION: Knutsford, tel 01565 632611

THE PUB: The Royal Oak, Alderley Edge

Getting to the start

Alderley Edge is a small and prosperous town along the A34 a little over a mile (1.6km) south of the larger town of Wilmslow. The start lies along the B5087, a busy shortcut linking Alderley Edge with Macclesfield.

Researched and written by:
Terry Marsh, Jon Sparks

WALK

Alderley Edge CHESHIRE

Beautiful Alderley Edge, a former copper mining area, is a place of myth and legend

left, and then about 140yds (128m) beyond a **National Trust sign**, in more open terrain now, bear right onto a track to a cross-path, with a field ahead. Turn right, through undergrowth, and just before another open field, go right, along the edge of the **wood**. Continue in a narrow strip of trees, with fields either side. Cross the road again and follow a track to the bare crest of **Castle Rock**.

3 Descend the steps to a level path. Go left 120yds (110m) to **Wizard's Well**. Return to the steps and continue below the crags on a terrace path, then up steps to join a higher path. Go left and almost immediately start descending again, with more steps in places. At the bottom cross a footbridge and climb again, levelling out briefly by the **Holy Well**. A few paces to its left go up over tree roots to where the path resumes. Climb shallow steps to a wider path, go left then turn right on to the rocky crest of **Stormy Point**.

4 Bear right above the rocks, and follow a wide track to a gate and vehicle track, and here go left. Follow signs '**Hare Hill**', down a steady descent with a small ravine at the bottom. Turn right and ascend again. Climb steps past tall beech trees, then

descend through **Clock House Wood**. Climb again to a National Trust sign and out into the open.

5 Go right, over a stile, across the waist of a field to another stile near **two ponds**. Go forward between the ponds and then left along the hedge to a stile hidden in a curve, then down a **fenced path**. Join a wider track and at the top go over a stile. Go right to another stile and then up to one more giving onto a grassy track. Cross a gravel track into another narrow fenced path and at its end turn left. Opposite the **National Trust works yard** go left through a gate for a shortcut to the car park or straight on to the tea room.

what to look for

Signs of mining activity can be seen in many places, most noticeably at Engine Vein and Stormy Point. There are deep covered shafts within the open working of Engine Vein. Most of what you see today was excavated in the 18th century, but there is evidence of much earlier working. The exposure of bare rock at Stormy Point is partly due to toxic minerals, though wear and tear by the feet of visitors plays a part too.

The Royal Oak

As there are no pubs on the walk, you'll have to drive to locate The Royal Oak, a popular and bustling pub near the centre of Alderley Edge. It offers a friendly atmosphere throughout the spacious and comfortably furnished dining areas. Lively locals bar with live sports television. On fine days, the adjacent garden and picnic tables make a perfect place to rest and refuel after the walk.

Food
Expect traditional pub food ranging from sandwiches and standard favourites to chilli, beef Madras, grilled Cajun chicken, steak and kidney pudding, T-bone steak, slow-roast lamb Henry and roast Sunday lunches; separate vegetarian menu.

Family facilities
The pub is family friendly, offering a children's menu and smaller portions. Good outdoor seating on a south-facing terrace and a large lawn where kids can play.

Alternative refreshment stops
The Wizard tea room, (open 1–5pm weekends and bank holidays), serves great cakes. The adjacent Wizard Inn is really a smart restaurant.

about the pub

The Royal Oak
28 Heyes Lane, Alderley Edge
Wilmslow, Cheshire SK9 7JY
Tel: 01625 584776

WALK

DIRECTIONS: turn right out of the car park and follow the B5087 into Alderley Edge. Turn right through the village centre, then turn right again into Heyes Lane; pub on the right

PARKING: 60

OPEN: all day; closed Sunday evening

FOOD: daily

BREWERY/COMPANY: Tetley

REAL ALE: changing guest ales

DOGS: allowed in the garden only

☞ Where to go from here
There's a 15th-century working watermill at Nether Alderley. The walled gardens and surrounding park of Hare Hill, probably best known for azaleas and rhododendrons, are 2 miles (3.2km) away (www.nationaltrust.org.uk). At Jodrell Bank Visitor Centre, a scientific and engineering wonder awaits you – the magnificent Lovell telescope, one of the largest radio telescopes in the world (www.jb.man.ac.uk).

Alderley Edge CHESHIRE

Down and up again to Mow Cop

26

WALK

Mow Cop

CHESHIRE/STAFFORDSHIRE

A walk that samples both the lush Cheshire Plain and the wilder ridges that overlook it.

Mow Cop Castle

Mow Cop is an odd place: its crooked streets seem to seek the steepest ways, and the village is as quirky as the castle that dominates it. Never a fortress, the castle is one of England's best-known and most conspicuous follies. The village sits on a sharp ridge, the last great outlier of the millstone grit. The view south is over the Potteries but north and west is the green expanse of the Cheshire Plain.

The walk starts level, passing the Old Man of Mow. This is a good place to pause and study the view before descending to the plain. The descent is steepest in the woods of Roe Park. Down on the level, you cross beneath the Manchester to Stoke-on-Trent railway line. Take care as high speed trains use this line. Just beyond, and on a parallel course, is the Macclesfield Canal, where the speed limit is a sedate 4mph (6.4kph). Though the general line of the canal was planned by Thomas Telford, the principal engineer was William Crossley.

On the way up again, be alert for a section past Limekiln Farm where the path hides in the undergrowth, then doubles back sharply. Higher up, there's a section with no clear path at all, but it's simply a matter of following the edge of a field.

Overall the ascent is less steep than the descent, but there's rough ground below the ridge crest. Here, if you so desire, you can walk with one foot in Cheshire and the other in Staffordshire. A path then threads a narrow belt of woodland before emerging and reaching an old quarry where in summer the level floor is alive with wild flowers.

the walk

1 Head towards the **castle**. Before reaching it, take a narrower path left to a road. Go right up this, then left, signposted 'Old Man of Mow' and 'South Cheshire Way'. Swing left, then right, then fork right on a narrow path past the **Old Man**. Rejoin the wider track, heading towards a **communications mast**.

View through a circular window hole at the folly known as Mow Cop Castle

The ruins of Mow Cop Folly, now owned by the National Trust

2h30 — **5.25 MILES** — **8.5 KM** — **LEVEL 1 2 3**

MAP:	OS Explorer 268 Wilmslow, Macclesfield & Congleton
START/FINISH:	National Trust car park directly below Mow Cop Castle; grid ref: SJ 857573
PATHS:	open fields and woodland paths, canal tow path, quiet lanes, short sections where path indistinct, 10 stiles
LANDSCAPE:	mostly farmland and deciduous woods on flanks of ridge, views from crest
PUBLIC TOILETS:	none on route
TOURIST INFORMATION:	Congleton, tel 01260 271095
THE PUB:	The Mow Cop Inn, Mow Cop

🚫 Some boggy sections, and lots of seasonal overgrowth can make the walk unsuitable for very young children – and, in summer, for anyone wearing shorts

Getting to the start

The ridge-top village of Mow Cop lies on the Cheshire-Staffordshire border south of Congleton and north east of Kidsgrove. It is most easily reached from the A34, and then by minor country lanes. The easiest way to find the car park at the start is to first find the Mow Cop Inn, and turn into Castle Road. At the top of the climb, go forward and take the first left immediately following a signposted track into the National Trust grounds of Mow Cop Castle.

Researched and written by:
Terry Marsh, Jon Sparks

Mow Cop

CHESHIRE/STAFFORDSHIRE

2 At a junction of footpaths go left. Follow the field edges downhill and continue descending in a **wood**. Where the footpath splits at a **waymark** in a tangle of holly bushes go left and into a field, then bear right. Skirt a **farm** then join a rough track. Keep heading downhill to join a surfaced lane. Bear left and cross the railway by a pedestrian underpass at **Ackers Crossing**.

3 Follow the lane to a wider road and turn right. Cross over a **canal bridge**, then go down steps and left, along the tow path. At **bridge No 81** go up to a lane and turn left, over the bridge.

4 Follow the narrow lane to **Fence Lane/ Wharf Lane** and go straight ahead up a track to **Limekiln Farm**. Take a track on the left just beyond a large barn. Keep low, along the edge of the wood, until the track bends right by a **waymark post** with yellow arrows.

5 Go left, pushing through undergrowth to **duckboards** and a stile. Turn right along a field edge. After 100yds (91m) there's another post. Descend sharp right then cross three, sometimes slippery, **plank bridges**. A narrow path heads uphill leading to a wider track, then to a **house**. Just as the track starts to descend, go right, up a track to a **stile**. Follow the left edge of a field alongside a wood (no path). After another stile go up the right-hand edge of the ensuing field. At a **waymark**, go right on a green track to a stile amid holly trees. Continue to another boundary; beyond is a large expanse of rougher ground with rushes and some gorse. A firm but frequently **obscure track** curves across this, though the last bit, to a stile, remains rough and rushy. Bear left up a drive to the road, then follow it right for 300yds (274m).

6 By the turning to **Roe Park Farm** a **Gritstone Trail sign** lurks under a beech tree, pointing the way into a narrow wood. The footpath roughly follows the upper margin of the wood, then emerges on the

what to look for

Mow Cop Folly was built in 1754 by John and Ralph Harding for the Wilbraham family of Rode Hall, about 3 miles (4.8km) to the west. It was probably used as an occasional summerhouse, but mostly served to enhance the view from Rode Hall. The hilltop was also the birthplace of Primitive Methodism: in May 1807 thousands gathered to launch a move back to simpler forms of worship. The term 'primitive' was not seen as derogatory: the usual contemporary term of abuse was 'Ranters'.

level floor of some old **quarry workings**. Climb left from a waymark to follow a path beside a wall below the **communications tower**, to rejoin the outward route near the **Old Man of Mow**.

The Mow Cop Inn

The stone-built Mow Cop Inn is close to the start of the walk, just below the hilltop on the Staffordshire side of the village. It's a cosy pub with an intimate feel and is essentially a locals' pub, but one that welcomes walkers. It does good-value English and Persian food and serves a tip-top pint of Greene King IPA. You can rest your legs at picnic benches on the raised front terrace on fine days.

Food
The straightforward pub menu offers tagliatelle Niçoise, home-made steak and kidney pie, moussaka and beef curry, alongside sandwiches and snacks. There are a few unusual Persian dishes, perhaps horesh lubia – lamb in a tomato sauce.

Family facilities
Families are welcome and children have their own menu.

Alternative refreshment stops
Nearby is the Egerton Arms at Astbury, just off the A34 near Congleton.

about the pub

The Mow Cop Inn
32 Congleton Road, Mow Cop
Stoke-on-Trent, Staffordshire ST7 3PJ
Tel: 01782 514117

DIRECTIONS: see Getting to the start
PARKING: 60
OPEN: evenings only Monday to Friday; lunchtime & evening Saturday; all day Sunday
FOOD: daily; all day Sunday
BREWERY/COMPANY: free house
REAL ALE: Greene King IPA
DOGS: not allowed inside

☛ Where to go from here
Little Moreton Hall at Scholar Green, which you can see from the ridge, is almost certainly the most celebrated half-timbered house in England. The house was built in stages between 1480 and 1580 and has hardly changed since then (www.nationaltrust.org.uk). If you head south to Burslem in Staffordshire, you can visit Ceramica, where children can discover the past, present and future of ceramics through interactive displays (www.ceramicauk.com).

Foulridge to Greenber Field

CYCLE

Foulridge   LANCASHIRE

An easy ride along the
Leeds to Liverpool Canal,
and a chance encounter
with stalactites and a ghost.

Above and below the ground
Kingfishers dart about along the canal, and
it is also worth keeping a wary eye open for
these arrows of iridescence. They like to
perch on branches overhanging the canal,
from which they dive into the water to catch
small fish.

Well worth a visit are the cellars of the
Anchor Inn at Salterforth, which have an
impressive array of 'straw' stalactites, and
some rather stunted stalagmites. It's
certainly not what you expect; nor the

flooded cellar; nor Joseph Widdup, who
hanged himself in the cellar, and whose
ghost still haunts the pub; not a fearful
spirit, just playful, as the barstaff may
well tell you.

the ride

1 Follow the **canal** to the locks at
Greenber Field, and then come back, is
about all that's really needed. The tow path
gives elevated views of the surrounding
countryside, and encounters no hindrance
until a gate complex is reached just past
The Anchor Inn at Salterforth.

2 Continue as far as **Bridge No. 153**, and
there, with care, emerge briefly onto

1h30	**8.25 MILES**	**13.2 KM**	**LEVEL 1**23

MAP: OS Explorer OL21 South Pennies

START/FINISH: Foulridge Wharf; grid ref: SD 888427

TRAILS/TRACKS: good tow path, with just a few cobbles in places

LANDSCAPE: mainly farmland, with rolling hills in the distance and little urbanisation

PUBLIC TOILETS: none on route

TOURIST INFORMATION: Barnoldswick (Colne), tel 01282 666704

CYCLE HIRE: Pedal Power, Waddington Road, Clitheroe, Lancashire BB7 2HJ, tel 01200 422066

THE PUB: The Anchor Inn, Salterforth

🛇 Care to be taken as whole ride is beside the canal

Getting to the start

Foulridge lies just over 1 mile (1.6km) north of Colne along the A56 to Skipton. In the centre of Foulridge, take the B6251, and follow signs for Foulridge Wharf. There is a small car park at the wharf.

Why do this cycle ride?

This is Pendle, a delightful mix of witchcraft and enchanting scenery, a place of ancient market towns and stone-built villages. But it so much more; bordering Yorkshire, there are extensive views framed by trees alongside the canal, and a pastoral loveliness. The ride is entirely flat all the way, and with only one brief road crossing to deal with as you switch sides of the canal, the miles simply slip by.

Researched and written by: Terry Marsh

Above: Riding along the tow path of the Leeds and Liverpool Canal at Greenber Field

a minor road in order to switch sides of the canal. Press on, passing some **light industrial units,** with an increasing amount of urbanisation as the route passes through the suburbs of **Barnoldswick**. This is short-lived, and soon farmland landscapes return, as the tow path heads for the locks at **Greenber Field**, once voted the best-kept locks in Britain.

3 The return route is simply back along the **tow path**, but perhaps calling in at The Anchor Inn on the way.

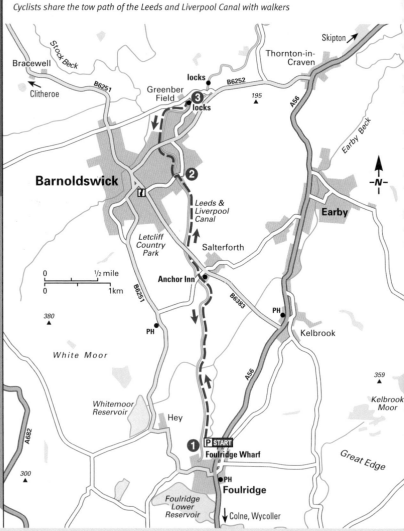

Cyclists share the tow path of the Leeds and Liverpool Canal with walkers

Skipton ↗

Bracewell

Stock Beck

Clitheroe

B6251

locks

B6252

Thornton-in-Craven

Greenber Field

❸ locks

195 ▲

A56

Earby Beck

–N–

Barnoldswick

❷

Leeds & Liverpool Canal

Earby

Letcliff Country Park

Salterforth

0   ½ mile

0   1km

B6251

Anchor Inn

B6383

PH

380 ▲

PH

Kelbrook

White Moor

359 ▲

Kelbrook Moor

Whitemoor Reservoir

Hey

A56

A682

❶ P START

Foulridge Wharf

Great Edge

300 ▲

PH

Foulridge

Foulridge Lower Reservoir

↓ Colne, Wycoller

The Anchor Inn

This friendly, homely and welcoming inn, together with the barn known as 'The Rough' at the rear, are amongst the oldest buildings in Salterforth, believed to date back to around 1655. It was the old 'travellers' rest', built on an old packhorse way, a salt road from Cheshire to Yorkshire. When the adjacent Leeds and Liverpool Canal was excavated between 1770 and 1816, the building became damp, so a new inn was erected, with the travellers' rest as the cellar. Today, there are four small, beamed rooms, and cellars that hold a fabulous stalactite formation, as well as a resident ghost, Joseph Widdup, whose family lived at the inn – he hanged himself in the cellar.

Food

Generous portions of traditional pub food range from basic snacks and Yorkshire puddings with various fillings to steak and kidney pie, gammon topped with onions and Wensleydale cheese, lamb Madras, and chicken Kiev.

Family facilities

The pub is a great stop-off point on the route, especially for children as there's a play area in the canalside garden and a genuine welcome awaits inside if the weather is poor. Young children have their own menu.

Alternative refreshment stops

Foulridge Tea Rooms serves hot meals and snacks and bakes fresh cakes and scones.

☞ Where to go from here

Wycoller Country Park at Trawden is renowned for its association with the Brontë sisters. There's a ruined 16th-century hall, a craft centre and tea room. Housed in the old Grammar School at Earby, the Museum of Yorkshire Dales Lead Mining contains a comprehensive collection of historical mining artefacts. Head east to Skipton and visit England's most complete medieval castle (www.skiptoncastle.co.uk).

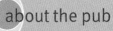

about the pub

The Anchor Inn
Salterforth Lane, Salterforth
Barnoldswick, Lancashire BB18 5TT
Tel: 01282 813186

DIRECTIONS: beside the canal at Salterforth Bridge, off the B6383 between the A56 at Kelbrook and Barnoldswick

PARKING: 40

OPEN: daily; all day

FOOD: daily; all day Sunday

BREWERY/COMPANY: Scottish & Newcastle

REAL ALE: John Smiths Cask, Ruddles Bitter, Courage Directors, Theakston Best

The Bridestone Rocks from Lydgate

Ancient tracks and gritstone outcrops, with terrific views of the steep-sided Cliviger Valley.

Unusual rock formations

The Long Causeway, between Halifax and Burnley, is an ancient trading route, possibly dating back to the Bronze Age. Crosses and waymarker stones helped to guide travellers across the moorland wastes, though most of them have been lost or damaged in the intervening years. Amazingly, Mount Cross has survived intact: a splendid, though crudely carved, example of the Celtic wheel-head design. Opinions differ about its age but it is certainly the oldest man-made artefact in the area, erected at least a thousand years ago.

The hills and moors to the north of Todmorden are dotted with gritstone outcrops. The impressive piles of Orchan Rocks and Whirlaw Rocks are both encountered on this walk. But the most intriguing rock formations are to be found at the Bridestones. One rock in particular has been weathered by wind and water into a teardrop shape, and stands on a base that looks far too slender to support its great weight. It resembles a rock in the North York Moors National Park, which is also known as the Bridestone.

The Cliviger Valley links two towns – Todmorden in West Yorkshire and Burnley in Lancashire – that expanded with the textile trade, and then suffered when that trade went into decline. The valley itself is narrow and steep-sided, in places almost a gorge. Into the cramped confines of the valley are shoe-horned the road, railway line, the infant River Calder and communities such as Portsmouth, Cornholme and Lydgate that grew up around the textile mills. The mills were powered by fast-flowing becks running off the steep hillsides. The valley is almost a microcosm of the Industrial Revolution: by no means beautiful, but full of character. This area is particularly well provided with good footpaths, some of them still paved with their original causey stones.

the walk

1 From the **post office** in Lydgate, walk up **Church Road**. At the end go right, down the drive towards a **house**. Take a path that passes to the right of this house and soon goes beneath the arch of a **railway viaduct**. Join a stony track, as you walk steeply uphill, the track is sunken, between walls. Where the walls end, the track gives access to open moorland. Keep right, along a track towards a farm. Keep left of the **farmhouse**, continuing along a walled track uphill. When you meet another walled track, go right towards a rocky outcrop on the first horizon. Beyond two gates you are on open moorland again: **Whirlaw Common**. Cross pasture on a section of paved causeway to arrive, via a gate, at **Whirlaw Stones**.

2 Keep to the **causeway** that bears right, below the stones, with panoramic views of the Cliviger Valley, Todmorden and, ahead, Stoodley Pike. Leave Whirlaw Common by a gate on to a walled path. Bear sharp left at a **farm**, on a stony track that follows a wall uphill. Bear right around the rocks, to join **Windy Harbour Lane**. You have a steep climb, before the road levels off to meet **Eastwood Road**. Go left here for

just 150yds (140m). Where the wall ends, take a stile on the left. A grassy path leads you to another fascinating collection of rocks, known as the **Bridestones**.

3 Continue across the Bridestones on a narrow green path through a landscape of scattered boulders, before turning right at a **waymark** to follow a path alongside a collapsed wall across rough terrain. Keep forward to meet a road, where you'll be greeted by **The Sportsman's Arms**.

4 Go left, along the road; you have a mile (1.6km) of level walking, passing the **Hawks Stones** on the right and a handful of houses, until you come to a minor road on the left. This is **Mount Lane**, signed to Shore

Top: View across the Bridestones
Below: A pond above Heptonstall

2h30 · **5 MILES** · **8 KM** · **LEVEL 1 2 3**

MAP: OS Explorer OL21 South Pennines
START/FINISH: roadside parking in Church Road, Lydgate; grid ref: SD 924256
PATHS: moorland and packhorse paths, some quiet roads, 3 stiles
LANDSCAPE: steep-sided valley and open moorland
PUBLIC TOILETS: none on route
TOURIST INFORMATION: Todmorden, tel 01706 818181
THE PUB: The Sportsman's Arms, Kebs
❶ Pub open evenings only Mon-Sat

Getting to the start
Lydgate is 1.5 miles (2.4km) out of Todmorden, on the A646, signposted Burnley.

Researched and written by:
Terry Marsh, John Morrison

28

WALK

Lydgate

WEST YORKSHIRE

125

what to look for

In geological terms, the South Pennines are largely made up of Millstone grit and coarse sandstone. Where the gritstone is visible, it forms rocky crags and outcrops, like those encountered on this walk. The typical landscape is moorland of heather and peat, riven by steep-sided valleys. Here, in the confines of the steep-sided Cliviger Valley, road, rail and river cross and re-cross each other like the flex of an old-fashioned telephone.

5 Detour past **Lower Intake Farm** on a path, soon enclosed by walls. At a cross-track, keep forward and 300yds (275m) beyond a small bridge over **Redmires Water**, look out for a gap stile on your right, by a gate between heavy stone gateposts. Follow a field path downhill, keeping a wall to your left. This grassy track takes you beneath another gritstone outcrop, known as **Orchan Rocks**.

6 Where the wall bears left, beyond the rocks, follow it downhill to a stile. You now join a **farm track** that takes a serpentine route downhill, through woodland. Your way is clear: down into the valley and back into Lydgate.

and Todmorden. Walk down this road and beyond a **farm** on the right, take a good track to the left, slightly downhill, heading towards **Lower Intake Farm**. Take a look at the **Mount Cross** in a field to your left.

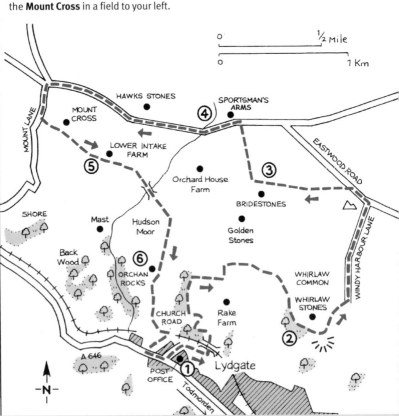

The Sportsman's Arms

The Sportsman's Arms is one of many isolated pubs in the South Pennines that seem to be situated 'miles from anywhere'. In fact they were built on old routes, and catered for customers on the move, such as drovers and the men who led the trains of packhorse ponies across the moorland tracks. The pub lies on the Long Causeway, now upgraded to a high-level road between Todmorden and Burnley and, these days, caters for motorists, local farmers and weary walkers in search of a hearty meal and a decent pint of beer. Regular local art exhibitions and live music on Fridays. Other than on Sundays, it is best to undertake this walk on a summer's afternoon and return to the pub for a meal as it only opens in the evening.

Food
Simple bar meals range from hot and cold sandwiches and ploughman's platters to home-made pies and lasagne.

Family facilities
Children are welcome and there's a children's menu as well as smaller portions of main menu dishes.

Alternative refreshment stops
The Staff of Life, on the main A646 at Lydgate, is another cosy 'real ale' pub where walkers get a warm welcome, but, again, only opens for lunch at weekends and Bank Holidays.

☞ Where to go from here
If you continue along the Long Causeway, you'll soon come to Coal Clough Windfarm. These huge wind turbines can be found on the crest of many a South Pennine hill, attracting strong winds and equally strong opinions. To some people they represent a sustainable future for energy, to others they are ugly intrusions in the landscape. In Towneley Park on the edge of Burnley, 16th-century Towneley Hall houses a gallery and museum as well as furnished period rooms (www.towneleyhall.org.uk).

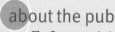

about the pub

The Sportsman's Arms
Kebs, Todmorden
West Yorkshire OL14 8SB
Tel: 01706 813449

DIRECTIONS: from Lydgate head away from Todmorden and turn right up Mount Lane, then right at the 3-way junction for the pub; see Point 3/4	
PARKING: 50	
OPEN: evenings only Monday to Saturday; all day Sunday	
FOOD: daily; all day Sunday	
BREWERY/COMPANY: Free House	
REAL ALE: Timothy Taylor Landlord, Thwaites Bitter, guest beers	
DOGS: allowed inside	

On the packhorse trail along Salter Rake

29

WALK

Warland   WEST YORKSHIRE

An invigorating moorland walk, punctuated by reservoirs, finishing off with a stretch of the Rochdale Canal.

Rocks, stones and reservoirs

Salter Rake is an old packhorse road which was used for transporting salt from the Cheshire salt mines across the Pennines. When these trading routes were first established, the Calder Valley was largely undrained. The teams of packhorse ponies, laden with pannier bags, would keep to the drier high ground, only descending into the valleys to cross rivers on the narrow stone bridges that are so typical of the area. Most of these causeways (or 'causeys') were paved with stones. More than three centuries after they were laid, these stones still fit snugly together as the pieces of a jigsaw. To judge from the way they are deeply 'dished', the stones have seen heavy use by countless horses' hooves.

Gritstone rocks and outcrops are familiar features throughout the South Pennines. The Basin Stone, an oddly-shaped rock looks – from one viewpoint – like a fish-tail.

Like many of the reservoirs you will encounter whilst walking in the South Pennines, the trio you see from this walk were built to supply water for a canal. The Rochdale Canal linked Manchester to the Calder and Hebble Navigation at Sowerby Bridge. By the 1920s there was little commercial traffic still using it, so the reservoirs were converted to join the water supply systems built to slake the thirst of East Lancashire's mill towns.

the walk

1 Walk to the right along the road for just 50yds (45m). Cross the road and take a track on the left, **Warland Gate End**, past some cottages. Cross the Rochdale Canal on a swing bridge and follow a lane uphill, between houses. At a sharp right-hand bend, by more houses, bear right and continue uphill. When the lane forks, keep right (forward) to **Calf Lee House** up on the moors. There, go through an **ornamental gate** (beware noisy dogs) to a gate and stile on the left. Cross the stile and go up to another house. Pass to the rear to locate a **stile**, and from it climb to a gate and stile above. Continue on a path above a stream gully to a gate, and there go forward towards Warland Reservoir. As you approach the **retaining wall** of the reservoir, you can follow the track on your right (or take a steeper short cut on the left) up to a **track** that follows the contours of the reservoir.

Above: Rochdale Canal at Warland
Below right: The Basin Stone above Warland

2h30 **5 MILES** **8 KM** **LEVEL 1 2 3**

WALK

MAP: OS Explorer OL21 South Pennines

START/FINISH: at pull-in for cars at roadside, near Bird I' th' Hand pub on A6033, between Todmorden and Littleborough; grid ref: SD 945201

PATHS: good paths and tracks throughout, 3 stiles

LANDSCAPE: open moorland, reservoirs and canalside

PUBLIC TOILETS: none on route

TOURIST INFORMATION: Todmorden, tel 01706 818181

THE PUB: Bird I' Th' Hand, Walsden

❶ There's a long uphill stretch to the first reservoir

Getting to the start

Warland is a straggling community along the Rochdale Canal and the A6033 between Todmorden and Littleborough. Approach by the A6033. Just south of the Bird i'th' Hand pub there is limited roadside parking, and the walk starts from here.

Researched and written by:
Terry Marsh, John Morrison

Warland

WEST YORKSHIRE

2 Walk left along this good, level track, with terrific views over Calderdale and East Lancashire. Cross a **bridge** at the northern end of the reservoir, and keep on the track as it follows a drainage channel.

3 When both track and channel wheel to the right, go left at a **stone bridge**, to follow a paved path to a smaller reservoir, **Gaddings Dam**. Walk along the left edge of the reservoir.

4 Bear half left at the far end of the reservoir, by a set of **stone steps**, on a clear path that soon passes close to the curiously shaped outcrop called the **Basin Stone**. Continue descending to a meeting of paths, marked with a small **waymarker post**.

5 Bear left here, on a path that's soon delineated by causeway stones; you are now following **Salter Rake**, an old packhorse

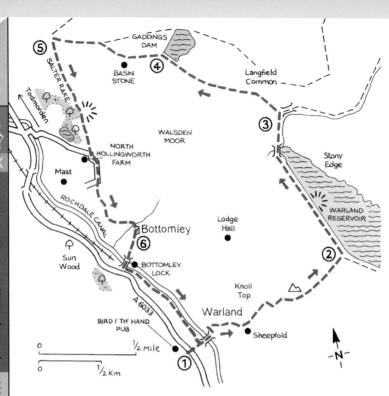

road. Enjoy excellent views over Walsden as you make a gradual descent, still across open moorland, then accompanying a wall. On approaching **houses**, go through a gate and between walls to join a metalled track past the houses and downhill. After 75yds (68m) you have a choice of routes. Keep left on a metalled track to another house.

what to look for

Steanor Bottom tollhouse is a small hexagonal building dating from the 1820s. You will find it on the main A6033 road, at a junction with a minor road, to the south of the Bird I' th' Hand pub. Tolls were collected here from any travellers wishing to use the new turnpike road. The tollhouse has been restored and retains its notice board presenting the tariff for all the different kinds of traffic, from sheep to carts.

Through a metal gate below the house, follow the **causeway stones** to the right, accompanying a wall (ignoring a more obvious track to the left). The footpath becomes sunken, between walls, as you descend and pass to the left of a **white-painted house**. The paved path takes you across a little **beck** and up into a small collection of houses, known as **Bottomley**. Go right here, down a metalled track, and bear immediately right again, through a gate, and on to a **cobbled, walled path** directly downhill, which takes you to the **Rochdale Canal**.

6 Cross the canal by the side of **Bottomley Lock**, and walk along the canal tow path. The fourth bridge you come to is the **swing bridge**. Go right here and back to the Bird i' th' Hand pub.

Bird I' Th' Hand

Your one source of refreshment on this walk is the Bird I' Th' Hand pub, where you park your car. It was built around 1825 to exploit the traffic using the turnpike road that had been opened just four years earlier. It's a homely, unpretentious locals' pub with a wide choice of traditional pub food, and is, of course, worth two in the bush...

Food
Other than sandwiches and traditional snacks, there's chicken balti, lambs' liver and onions, sweet and sour chicken, fisherman's pie, haddock and chips, and Cumberland sausage, mash and onion gravy.

Family facilities
A friendly welcome awaits families who are welcome in the eating area and a children's menu is available for younger diners.

about the pub

Bird I' Th' Hand
Rochdale Road, Walsden
Todmorden, West Yorkshire OL14 6UH
Tel: 01706 378145

DIRECTIONS: see Getting to the Start	
PARKING: 30	
OPEN: daily	
FOOD: daily	
BREWERY/COMPANY: Enterprise Inns	
REAL ALE: none served	
DOGS: not allowed inside	

Alternative refreshment stops
In nearby Todmorden you will find a good range of pubs and cafés.

☞ Where to go from here
South east of Walsden, just off the A68 is a short, steep track over the Pennine watershed of Blackstone Edge. This elaborately paved path, about 13ft (4m) wide and with a stone channel down the middle, is marked on the Ordnance Survey map as a Roman road, but opinions about its origins are divided.

It doesn't resemble other known roads of that period. Nor, however, is it like the paved packhorse causeways that criss-cross the South Pennines. One thing is sure: if it is Roman, it's one of the best-preserved examples in the country.

Around Lyme Park

A circuit of the attractive grounds of Lyme Park, a fine country house.

Lyme Park

It's the classic English stately home: a medieval manor house that was gradually transformed into a large elegant Palladian mansion, full of antique furniture, tapestries, carvings and clocks. Outside, there are formal gardens (including an Edwardian Rose Garden and an Orangery), plus open moorland and parkland that is home to red and fallow deer. In 1946 the house and park were donated to the National Trust.

This circular walk offers ever-changing views of Lyme Park. From tree-lined avenues and open meadows to the tiny reservoirs of the Bollinhurst Valley. The rough moors to the south and east offer the best vantage points – it is said you can see seven counties from the top of Sponds Hill – but don't forget to examine things closer to hand. Near Bowstonegate is a small enclosure containing the Bow Stones, thought to be the middle sections of late-Saxon crosses which may have been ancient boundary markers. The sole surviving cross head is now to be found in the courtyard at Lyme Park.

Lyme Park and its mansion was the location for the BBC production of Pride and Prejudice *in 1994*

the walk

1 With the lake on your right and the house on your left leave the car park by the **drive** and, as it begins to bend away to the right, turn left for a wide track through a gate signposted **'Gritstone Trail'**. Follow this through **Knightslow Wood**, negotiating several ladder stiles, until you emerge on **moorland**.

2 Go straight ahead/left on the main track as it climbs the moorland, aiming for the small **TV masts** on the skyline. At the top cross another stile and a short field to emerge at the end of a surfaced lane by the **Bow Stones**.

3 Turn left and follow the lane downhill until you reach its junction with another road, opposite the driveway to a **hotel**. Turn left and walk up the drive of **Cock Knoll Farm**. When you get to the buildings head right, across the farmyard, as indicated by footpath signs. At the far side, go through a gate and down the left-hand side of a field.

4 As you draw level with a small thicket in the shallow valley on the left, go over a **stile** and through the trees. Out on the other side, head right across the bottom of a field. Clear **waymark posts** now point you through several rough fields to a walled lane on the far side.

5 Once you are on the lane turn right and continue over **Bollinhurst Bridge**. (If you turn left you can take a short cut back to the house from here via **East Lodge**.) Beyond **Millennium Wood** you reach a junction of tracks. Go through the gate on the left and

3h30 · **5.5 MILES** – **8.8 KM** · **LEVEL 1**23

MAP: OS Explorer OL1 Dark Peak

START/FINISH: Lyme Park, off A6 (free to National Trust members); grid ref: SJ 964823

PATHS: generally firm, field tracks can be slippery if wet, 12 stiles

LANDSCAPE: rolling parkland and fields, some moorland

PUBLIC TOILETS: by Old Workshop Tea Room, near main car park

TOURIST INFORMATION: Macclesfield, tel 01625 504114

THE PUB: The Ram's Head, Buxton Road West

❶ The undulations and cumulative ascent would be tiring for very young children

Getting to the start

Access to the park is from the A6 (Stockport–Disley) road, just 0.5 mile (800m) west of Disley.

Researched and written by:
Terry Marsh, Andrew McCloy

WALK

Lyme Park CHESHIRE

take a grassy track, half left, signposted to **North Lodge.**

6 Descend the right-hand side of a rough field to the woodlands at the bottom. The path now goes over several stiles as it skirts round **Bollinhurst Reservoir** – keep close to the wall on your left. A newly laid, gated gravel path takes you around the side of **Cockhead Farm**, and then continues across another field and down a shaded grassy lane. At the end of the lane turn right, on to a surfaced drive, to reach **North Lodge**.

7 Go through the **pedestrian gate** at the lodge, then turn left and walk along the main drive for about 250yds (229m). Take the obvious footpath up the hillside on your

what to look for

The curious hilltop folly known as The Cage is one of Lyme Park's most visible landmarks. An elegant three-floored structure, it was built around 1735 as a banqueting house, but since then has been variously used as an observation tower for watching the stag hunt, as a lodging for the park's gamekeepers, and even as a temporary prison for poachers. After falling derelict, it has undergone restoration and is occasionally open to visitors.

left, between a short avenue of trees, to reach the top of the open, grassy ridge. Head for the unmistakable hilltop folly known as **The Cage**, then continue straight on to return to the house and car park.

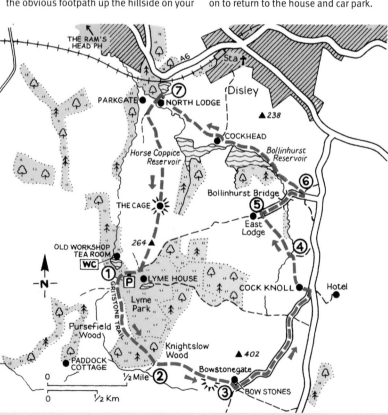

The Ram's Head

Located at an important highway junction on the A6 in the village of Disley, the Ram's Head is a bright, friendly and bustling pub, with elegant Georgian fireplaces and neo-contemporary chandeliers hang from the ceiling. A popular refreshment stop for A6 travellers, it is also a convenient post-walk destination as it is close to Lyme Park. Refresh and refuel at all times of the day with good cask ales and enjoyable, traditional bar food that includes Sunday roast lunches.

Food

From an extensive menu choose lasagne, Cajun salmon salad, lamb cutlets, chicken pie or a mixed grill, or something lighter such as freshly made sandwiches.

Family facilities

Children are welcome inside and young children have their own menu. The large enclosed rear garden and patio are perfect for summer sipping.

Alternative refreshment stops

The Ale Cellar Restaurant inside the house serves a range of 'traditional meals and historic menus' and is licensed, while the Old Workshop Tea Room, located near the car park by the large millpond and open daily in season, operates on a self-service basis and has a decent range of snacks and light refreshments.

☛ Where to go from here

It would be a shame not to visit the house itself, with its splendid gardens (www.nationaltrust.org.uk). Otherwise the nearby Macclesfield Canal provides a pleasant corridor for recreation, and not just for water-borne users. It forms part of the Cheshire Ring Canal Walk, a 97-mile (156km) circular route around Greater Manchester incorporating the tow paths of six historic canals, including the Peak Forest and the Trent & Mersey. The stretch past Lyme Park, between Macclesfield and Marple, is particularly rural and peaceful.

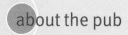

about the pub

The Ram's Head

Buxton Road West, Disley
Stockport, Cheshire, SK12 2AE
Tel: 01663 767909

DIRECTIONS: turn left out of the gates to the park, follow the main road to Disley to locate the pub at a road junction, near traffic lights

PARKING: 80

OPEN: daily; all day

FOOD: daily; all day

BREWERY/COMPANY: Tetley

REAL ALE: Boddingtons, Bass, John Smiths

DOGS: not allowed inside

Middlewood Way

Leafy railway trackbed and canal tow path combine in this ancient transport circuit.

Poynton Coppice

Poynton Coppice is classed as ancient semi-natural woodland, and as such is a rarity. It has never been ploughed up or used for any purpose other than the production of timber. Only one-fifth of British woodland, has this select status, and Poynton Coppice has not been disturbed since 1945, when the trees were cut off at ground level and left to grow back from the base. As a result, the wood contains trees that are all of the same age. In the coppice, you get plants such as wood sorrel, woodruff and yellow archangel, all ancient woodland indicators, which demonstrate that the woodland has been established for a long time.

Coppicing used to be the most common form of woodland management, and relied upon the rotational cutting of regrowth to produce both underwood (the coppice) and large timber (standards). This not only provided medieval man with a continuous supply of wood in different sizes, but also produced woodland species with continuous woodland conditions in suitably different stages, and particularly a balance between light and shade.

the ride

1 Leave the car park by locating the path (near the play area) that leads up wide-spaced steps on the nearside of the viaduct to reach the **old railway trackbed**. You will need to carry or push bicycles up this short section. Once at the top, set off northwards along a delightful route, flanked by mixed woodland

Above: The Macclesfield Canal

2h00 — **8 MILES** — **12.7 KM** — **LEVEL 123**

MAP: OS Explorer 268 Wilmslow, Macclesfield and Congleton

START/FINISH: Adlington Road, Bollington; grid ref: SJ 930780

TRAILS/TRACKS: old railway trackbed in good condition and canal towpath

LANDSCAPE: rural Cheshire, farmland rising to minor hills to the east

PUBLIC TOILETS: at the start and at Nelson Pit visitor centre

TOURIST INFORMATION: Macclesfield, tel 01625 504114

CYCLE HIRE: none locally

THE PUB: The Miners' Arms, Adlington

❶ One steep downhill section, towpath is narrow in places with some seasonal overhanging vegetation. Steps to negotiate.

Getting to the start

Bollington lies about 2.5 miles (4km) north east of Macclesfield. Leave the A523 for the B5090 and travel through the centre of Bollington. Look for signs to 'Middlewood Way', one of which directs you into Adlington Road. The car park, and an adjacent children's adventure play area, is about 200 yards (180m) down the road.

Why do this cycle ride?

This is a ride of contrasts. On the one hand, there is the pleasure of cycling along a renovated railway trackbed – the Middlewood Way – through light mixed woodland, and on the other, a delightful return along the towpath of the Macclesfield Canal, which has glorious views over the foothills of the Peak District National Park.

Researched and written by: Terry Marsh

2 **Poynton Coppice** is worth a brief detour on foot (see below). After that, as before, the on-going route description is easy, as the ride simply follows the trackbed as far as **Bridge 15**. Here, leave the trackbed, and go up (dismount here) to cross a minor road and reach the **Nelson Pit visitor centre**.

3 From the visitor centre, cycle up towards the car park, and there go through a narrow gap to join the tow path of the **Macclesfield Canal**. Turn right, and immediately cross a large, cobbled humpback bridge, and go beneath Bridge 15 to continue along the tow path. There are a couple of short sections between **Bridges 18 and 19** where the tow path dips briefly to the water's edge, and, with young children, it may be safer to dismount.

4 Leave the tow path at **Bridge 26**, by climbing up steps on the right to meet a minor road. Turn right, and follow the road as it drops very steeply to the northern edge of **Bollington**, and back to the Adlington Road car park.

Below: A sign made from a wheel on the Middlewood Way

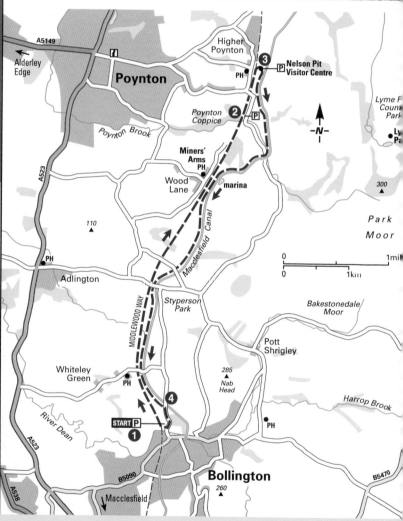

The Miners' Arms

big, bright and modern village pub that
s well organised and set up to attract
nd entertain families. The spacious and
iry bars and dining area are adorned
ith old farming memorabilia. Open fires
dd warmth and character to the place,
nd the friendly welcome to families
xtends to organising family fun days
ith children's entertainers. It is also
opular with locals, walkers and cyclists,
he latter having the use of bike racks in
he car park.

ood

raditional pub menus include a wide
ange of light meals, beef and ale pie,
amb shoulder, lasagne, oven bakes (lamb
avarin and beef and beer casserole), and
sweet and sour chicken.

amily facilities

n addition to the above, you'll find a
hildren's menu, high chairs, family quiz
ights, and a large garden with an
dventure play area.

Alternative refreshment stops

Picnic sites along the Middlewood Way.

**☞ Where to go from
here**

Magnificent Lyme Park,
the largest house in
Cheshire, has been the
home of the Legh family
for 600 years and
featured as Pemberley in
the BBC's production of
Pride and Prejudice. Visit
the house and explore
the historic gardens and
1,400 acre park

about the pub

The Miners' Arms
Wood Lane North, Adlington
Macclesfield, Cheshire SK10 4PF
Tel: 01625 872731
www.minersarms.info

DIRECTIONS: Wood Lane is located east off
the A523 between Adlington and Poynton,
just 150 yds (135m) off the cycle route

OPEN: daily; all day

FOOD: daily; all day

BREWERY/COMPANY: Spirit Group

REAL ALE: Boddingtons, guest beers

(www.nationaltrust.org.uk). Nether Alderley
Mill near Alderley Edge dates from the 15th-
century and features original Elizabethan
timberwork and Victorian machinery, and
is in full working order.

Tegg's Nose meadows

The set-piece comes early and the rest of the walk unfolds gentler views.

Tegg's Nose

The breezy crest of Tegg's Nose, with its interesting quarry remains and fine views, is as far as many visitors get, but a longer walk around the area sets it in context and delivers much greater variety.

While quarries are a feature of many walks in Cheshire and Lancashire, Tegg's Nose is particularly interesting. Examples of preserved machinery, accompanied by explanatory signs, give an insight into how the stone was worked. Beyond the quarries the track swings round the end of the hill – the 'Nose' itself. The steep slopes add depths to the view south, down to Langley where streams combine to form the River Bollin and across to Macclesfield Forest and Shutlingsloe. The descent looks west, over Macclesfield and the Cheshire Plain.

The steep descent takes you quickly down into woods. Among the beech and oak you'll also find hornbeam. This is often mistaken for beech but its leaves are longer, more pointed and have serrated edges. After crossing Tegg's Nose Reservoir you start to climb again, in the small valley of Walker Barn Stream. Although much of the ascent is on a tarmac lane, it only serves a handful of farms and is usually quieter than the tracks on Tegg's Nose itself. No cars, very few walkers and a handful of bikes seem to be the order of the day.

Once over the A537 there's a more level interlude. A bend in the track gives a view down into the valley of the River Dean, sheltered by Kerridge Hill. The village of

Rainow was once a silk and cotton weaving centre and a staging point on a medieval packhorse route conveying salt from the Cheshire mines. The A537 has to be crossed again but the final stretch is a pleasure, over easy slopes where, in summer, you're likely to find good old-fashioned meadows. High walls, with high stiles, separate them.

the walk

1 From the car park entrance a well-surfaced path, almost level, leads off left. At a gate into the **country park**, go left up steps, past spoil heaps and then below a quarry face. The path continues past some old machinery and explanatory signs, then above the deep bowl of a **quarry**. Keep left at the next fork, and follow the main track as it swings round the end of the hill.

2 Go past one stile then left over a second, on the **Tegg's Nose Trail**. Descend with stone flags on steeper sections, then mostly on grass and down

A picnic site with a wonderful view over Tegg's Nose

2h30 — 5 MILES — 8 KM — LEVEL 1 2 3

MAP: OS Explorer OL24 White Peak

START/FINISH: Tegg's Nose Country Park, on Buxton Old Road; grid ref: SJ 950733

PATHS: mostly on tracks and quiet lanes, some field paths, 15 stiles

LANDSCAPE: steep green hills and valley slopes are main backdrop

PUBLIC TOILETS: at car park

TOURIST INFORMATION: Macclesfield, tel 01625 504114

THE PUB: The Leather's Smithy, Langley

🛈 A significant amount of up and down may make this walk tiring for very young children

Getting to the start

Tegg's Nose Country Park lies along the old Buxton Road out of Macclesfield, which is reached by diverting from the A537 either from the Macclesfield end or from Walker Barn, if coming from the Buxton direction. The car park is pay and display.

Researched and written by:
Terry Marsh, Jon Sparks

through a wood to a small car park. Follow the track across the dam of **Tegg's Nose Reservoir** then left up another track alongside the water. (To visit the **Leather's Smithy** at this stage, follow the Gritstone Trail ahead, across the dam of Bottoms Reservoir, and turn left along the road for 0.5 mile/800m. Return to Tegg's Nose Reservoir). At a fork keep left, down to cross a stream.

3 The track climbs then levels out at a stile just above **Clough House**. Walk on to a lane and turn left up it. Follow it up to cross the busy A537.

4 Almost exactly opposite are a stile and a track down the hill. Where it starts to bend away right, keep straight on down by a stone wall, over the stream and left to a stile. Go left on a pleasant grassy path, just above a **collapsed wall**, then a level terrace path under beech trees. Keep straight on through the former **Hordern Farm**, and over a rise until the track bends right, becoming surfaced.

5 Go sharp left over a **wooden stile** and along the edge of a field. From a second stile, in the field corner, bear left alongside a wall to a stile above a steeper slope. Drop straight down to the stream, climb left around holly trees to another stile. Go straight up past a **barn** and, from a stile above, bear slightly right and up to **Bull Hill Lane**. Go left to the junction with the A537.

6 Go left up the main road for about 50yds (46m), cross and go up steps in the wall to a gate and **Gritstone Trail sign**. Follow the right edge of the field. The line is now almost straight over a series of stiles, with Gritstone Trail signs all the way, first

what to look for

An obvious difference between the Cheshire Plain and the surrounding hills is in the field boundaries. Hedgerows are widespread on the plain. In the hills, with ready access to stone, dry-stone walls are the norm. Dry-stone walling is a skilled and time-consuming occupation, but a well-built wall may last for a century or more.

climbing then levelling out and finally descending before meeting **Buxton Old Road**. Go right and down, back to the start

The Leather's Smithy

Alternative refreshment stops
There may be an ice-cream van at the car park during summer months.

☞ Where to go from here
Macclesfield was a centre for the silk industry, and preserves much of this history at Paradise Mill, a working silk mill until 1981, with restored hand looms in their original location. Macclesfield's Silk Museum in the Heritage Centre tells the story of silk in the town through a colourful audio-visual programme, exhibitions, textiles, garments, models and room settings (www.silk-macclesfield.org).

Beautifully located pub, overlooking Macclesfield Forest and Ridgegate Reservoir with a country park to the rear, hence very popular with the local walking fraternity. Dating from the 18th century and recently refurbished and extended, the pub commemorates William Leather, a licensee in the early 1800s, and the building's one-time use as a forge. There are great views from sunny front benches and the stone-flagged bar and carpeted dining rooms are cosy and welcoming on wild winter days. Rooms are traditionally furnished and feature warm open fires, interesting guest beers and farm cider.

Food
Options range from soup, sandwiches and snacks such as big bowls of mussels and ploughman's lunches, to lamb shank with mint jus, fresh Dover sole, pheasant in whisky, and steak and ale pie.

Family facilities
Children of all ages are welcome in the family room and smaller portions from the main menu are available.

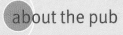

about the pub

The Leather's Smithy
Clarke Lane, Langley
Macclesfield, Cheshire SK11 0NE
Tel: 01260 252313
www.leatherssmithy.co.uk

DIRECTIONS: from the car park, turn left then left again for Langley. At the T-junction in the village turn left and keep left at a fork and follow the lane for 0.75 mile (1.2km). Pub opposite Ridgate Reservoir

PARKING: 25

OPEN: daily

FOOD: daily

BREWERY/COMPANY: free house

REAL ALE: Theakston Best, Marston's Pedigree, Courage Directors, guest beer

DOGS: allowed in the garden only

From Wildboarclough to Macclesfield Forest

A circular walk exploring the old and new Macclesfield Forest and the mini Matterhorn of Shutlingsloe.

Macclesfield Forest

The Royal Forest of Macclesfield was once the preserve of the nobility, an extensive hunting ground for the royal court where deer and boar were keenly sought out. There were severe penalties for poachers – the name of the isolated hilltop pub that the walk visits is called the Hanging Gate.

Near the start of the walk is the equally descriptive Crag Inn, tucked away above Clough Brook at Wildboarclough. Looming above Wildboarclough is the coned peak of Shutlingsloe, which at 1,659ft (505m) offers a full 360 degrees of panoramic views over Cheshire, Staffordshire and Derbyshire. Especially prominent is Tegg's Nose, a gritstone outcrop to the north above the dark green conifers of the forest. This modern plantation produces timber, although native broadleaved trees such as rowan, oak and silver birch have been planted in recent years to break up the regimented rows of spruces and larches and to encourage wildlife. Walkers are welcome to explore the forest's many path and tracks that climb the often steep hillsides. Look out for the occasional wooden sculpture, and wildlife such as crossbills and woodpeckers, stoats and foxes. The heronry in the larch trees on the eastern shore of Trentabank Reservoir is th largest in the Peak District.

the walk

3h30 · **7 MILES** · **11.3 KM** · **LEVEL 123**

1 Walk along the road for 440yds (400m) to the **Crag Inn**, then at the foot of its drive go over a stile on the left for a path across a sloping field. This maintains its direction through successive fields (each with a ladder stile) until finally you reach the **farm drive** at the top. Turn left and walk along this to the lane.

2 Turn right and walk along the lane as far as **Greenway Bridge**. Go over a stile on the right and follow the path beside the stream, until it crosses it in order to veer left, up **Oaken Clough**. Keep to the bottom of this little valley, past a ruined stone shelter, and as it rises continue to its far head, near a **small pond**. Turn right on to a private drive and then go almost immediately left for a **wall-side path** uphill.

3 At the top go over a stile and out across **moorland** on a clear grassy track. Maintain your direction until you reach a stile on the far side. Go over this and descend a sunken, fenced track to emerge opposite **The Hanging Gate** pub.

4 Turn right and follow the **road** for a mile (1.6km), keeping straight on at the junction where the road bends sharply left. Ignore another turning on the left, until finally the lane turns right, into **Macclesfield Forest**, where there's a wide gate on the right.

A map of Trentabank for walkers to consult as they look across the reservoir

MAP: OS Explorer OL24 White Peak

START/FINISH: lay-by at Brookside, on lane 1 mile (1.6km) south of Wildboarclough; grid ref: SJ 980681

PATHS: sloping field paths, lanes and easy forest tracks, steep hillside, 20 stiles

LANDSCAPE: rough pasture, angular hills, plus large tracts of woodland

PUBLIC TOILETS: at Macclesfield Forest Visitor Centre

TOURIST INFORMATION: Macclesfield, tel 01625 504114

THE PUB: The Hanging Gate, Higher Sutton

❶ This is a long walk with considerable height gain, which makes it unsuitable, or very tiring at the least, for younger children

Getting to the start

Macclesfield Forest lies about 3 miles (4.8km) south east of the town, and the start near Wildboarclough is best reached along quiet lanes through Langley, off the A523 just south of Macclesfield.

Researched and written by:
Terry Marsh, Andrew McCloy

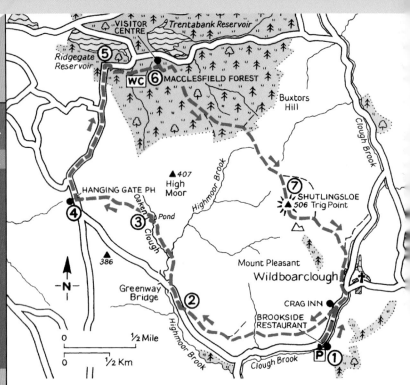

5 Don't go through the main gate but instead go over the **stile** to the left, signposted 'Shutlingsloe/Trentabank', and follow the footpath that runs parallel with the lane. After dropping down to a newly planted area cross the **footbridge** and at the junction of tracks near the **wood sculpture** carry straight on (still signposted 'Shutlingsloe'). At the far end turn right, or for the visitor centre and toilets at **Trentabank**, turn left.

6 Walk up the wide **forest drive** and go left at a fork, then at the far end turn right for a long but quite easy **gravel track** up through the trees. At the top go through a gate and continue straight on, then turn right to leave the forest for a stone-flagged path across the open moorland to the distinctive top of **Shutlingsloe**.

7 From the summit descend the eroded track down the steep eastern slope of the hill, until eventually you turn right on to the **open farm drive**. Follow this all the way down to the road at the bottom and turn right to return to the car park.

what to look for

At first glance Wildboarclough might seem a sleepy and uneventful place, but in fact it was once a hive of industrial activity. Two centuries ago Clough Brook was harnessed to provide power for local textile mills, and a calico-printing factory known as Crag Works was established. Stanley Pool, still evident behind the church, was constructed to power the works, but nothing remains of the 30ft (9m) water wheel.

The Hanging Gate

First licensed over 300 years ago, this family-run old drovers' inn is set high on a ridge with a splendid, sunny front terrace affording spectacular views over the Cheshire Plain towards the Welsh mountains. Inside, there are three cosy rooms on different levels, (all enjoy the view), and all have wonderful winter coal fires, traditional furnishings, and attractive prints on the walls. Add tip-top beer from Hyde's brewery and homely pub food and it's no wonder that this rural pub is popular amongst the local walking fraternity.

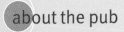

about the pub

The Hanging Gate
Higher Sutton, Macclesfield
Cheshire SK11 0NG
Tel: 01260 252238

DIRECTIONS: from A54 south west of Buxton turn off at Fourways Motel, following signs to Langley. From A523 south of Macclesfield, follow signs for Sutton Lanes End, then Wincle and Wildboarclough signs; see Point **3/4**

PARKING: 50

OPEN: daily; all day

FOOD: daily

BREWERY/COMPANY: Hyde's Brewery

REAL ALE: Hyde's Bitter, Jekyll's Gold, Tickety Boo & seasonal ales

DOGS: not allowed inside

Food
Bar food ranges from home-made soups, sandwiches and savoury prawn pancakes to freshly battered cod and chips, gammon and pineapple, lamb chops and rib-eye steak.

Family facilities
Children are allowed in the eating area of the bar where youngsters can order from their own menu.

Alternative refreshment stops
The other decent pub on the route is the Crag Inn at Wildboarclough, which also serves hot and cold meals and snacks every lunchtime and evening. The Brookside Restaurant, by the car park at the start/finish of the walk, is open most weekends for meals and light snacks.

☛ Where to go from here
Head across the border into Derbyshire and visit Pooles Cavern in Buxton Country Park. Take a 45-minute guided tour through the chambers of this impressive natural cavern containing thousands of crystal formations (www.poolescavern.co.uk). Discover more about the silk industry in Macclesfield by visiting the Silk Museum in the town's Heritage Centre, or enjoy a tour of Paradise Mill, a working silk mill until 1981 (www.silk-macclesfield.org).

A loop from Hebden Bridge

Textile history from cottage industry to the mills of bustling Hebden Bridge.

Calderdale Cloth Industry

This walk links the little town of Hebden Bridge with the old hand-weaving village of Heptonstall. The hill village of Heptonstall is by far the older settlement and was an important textile centre when Hebden Bridge was little more than a river crossing. Heptonstall's importance waned during the Industrial Revolution.

As soon as spinning and weaving developed on an industrial scale, communities sprang up near running water. The town of Hebden Bridge was established at the meeting of the Calder and Hebden Water. The 16th-century bridge that gives the town its name is still there. The town's speciality was cotton: mostly hard-wearing fustian and corduroy. With Hebden Bridge hemmed in by hills, and the mills occupying much of the available land on the valley bottom, the workers' houses had to be built up the steep slopes.

Jumble Hole Clough is a typical steep-sided, wooded valley. Though tranquil now, this little valley had four mills exploiting the fast-flowing beck. You can see remains of all these mills; but the most intriguing relic is Staups Mill, now an evocative ruin.

the walk

1 From the centre of Hebden Bridge, walk along Holme Street to the **Rochdale Canal**. Go right to follow the tow path beneath two bridges, past the **Stubbing Wharf pub** and beneath a railway bridge.

Go past **Rawden Mill Lock No. 12** and just before the next bridge, bear right and join a track right, to the A646.

2 Cross the road and bear right for just 75yds (68m) to take **Underbank Avenue**, on the left, through an arch. Bear left again, past houses, to where another road comes through the viaduct. Go right on a track (signed **Jack Bridge** and part of the Pennine Bridleway) past a mill, and follow the beck up into the woodland of **Jumble Hole Clough**. As the Pennine Bridleway bears right, leave it and go left over a bridge to a hairpin bend, climb steeply. When the track wheels left, keep ahead, now above the beck, and taking care on slippery rocks. Take a gate and cross the bottom of a field, to re-enter woodland. Keep ahead uphill, to a gap in a fence. Walk downhill, past the ruins of **Staups Mill**, then steeply up to cross a bridge. Take steps and cross a field to a waymark. Keep left, following a wall to a gate in front of **Hippins**.

3 Join the **Calderdale Way**, bearing right up a track between farm buildings to a stile. Follow a path to the next stile; then between a fence and a wall. Cross the track to **Apple Tree Farm**, to follow a line of causeway stones across three more stiles, passing to the right of a cottage. Cross the field to a gate at the right corner, then follow a causeway over a stile, and along a track to **Blackshaw Head**.

4 Go right, along the road, for 10yds (9m), to take a gate on the left. Bear half right across the field to a stile, then follow the right edge of the next field. Cross

our more fields, and stiles, to a gate. Go
left down a path, to **Shaw Bottom**. Keep left
of the house to a metalled track.

5 Go right, along the track (or left for the
New Delight Inn). When the track bears
left, keep ahead on a stony track. Look out
for a **small marker post**; go left here,
steeply down steps, and cross **Colden
Water** on a stone bridge. Climb up the other
side, to follow a causeway to the right, at
the top of woodland. Take care while
walking the causeway, the edge is often
concealed by bracken. At a metal gate turn
left and right to keep following the
causeway stones; your route is clear,
through gates and stiles, as **Heptonstall**
comes into view. Keep right at a track
junction, pass to the left of a **house**. At the
next crossing of tracks, by a bench, keep
straight ahead, on a walled path downhill.
Keep left at the next fork to meet a road.

*The Rochdale Canal runs past old mill buildings
at Hebden Bridge*

3h00 — **5.5 MILES** — **8.8 KM** — **LEVEL 123**

WALK

Hebden Bridge

WEST YORKSHIRE

MAP: OS Explorer OL21 South Pennines

START/FINISH: pay car parks in Hebden
Bridge; grid ref: SD 992272

PATHS: good paths, but seasonally
overgrown, 10 stiles

LANDSCAPE: steep-sided valleys, fields
and woodland

PUBLIC TOILETS: Hebden Bridge and
Heptonstall

TOURIST INFORMATION: Hebden Bridge,
tel 01422 843831

THE PUB: New Delight Inn, Blackshaw

🛈 Slippery rocks, concealed causeway
edges, proximity to cliff edges, steep cobbled
descent. For older, experienced children only

Getting to the start

Hebden Bridge is a lively and thriving small
town along the River Calder just 6 miles
(9.7km) west of Halifax along the A646 to
Todmorden.

Researched and written by:
Terry Marsh, John Morrison

6 Go left here, uphill. Just before the road bears left, take a gap in the wall to the right. From here your path meanders through **woodland** (it's a bit of a scramble and slippery in places). Emerge from the woodland, and follow a wall to and cross the top of **Hell Hole Rocks**: take care here as the path passes close to the cliff edge in places.

7 Bear left at a **wall-end**, and cross an access road. Just before the next access road, turn right (at a signpost) onto a walled track to the **Social and Bowling Club**. Go right, on a walled path and follow the wall to your left, downhill, soon through a spur of woodland and on leaving the woodland, bear left, downhill, parallel with a **wall** on the left eventually to meet a lane head. Turn right and walk down to a road junction. Go left for 40yds (37m) and take the paved track right. This is the **Buttress**, taking you steeply down into Hebden Bridge.

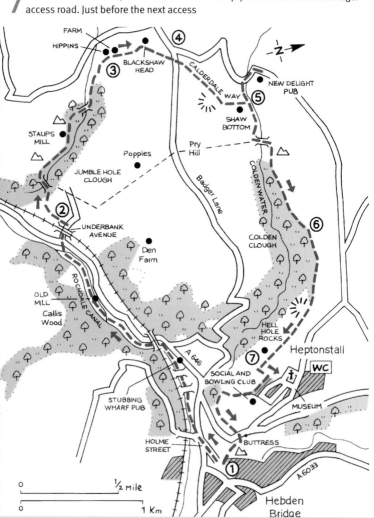

New Delight Inn

New Delight Inn stands in a lovely setting on the moors above Hebden Bridge and is conveniently situated at the halfway point of the walk. Good beer, imaginative food and stone-flagged floors make it the ideal spot for a meal, as do the views from the garden on fine summer days.

Food

Bar food takes in light bites like sandwiches and ploughman's lunches, alongside lamb shank, home-made vegetable and parsley pie, chilli, barbeque ribs, and beef in black bean sauce.

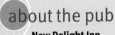

about the pub

New Delight Inn
New Shaw Lane, Jack Bridge
Blackshaw, Hebden Bridge
West Yorkshire HX7 7HT
Tel: 01422 846178

DIRECTIONS: north west of Hebden Bridge; take Heptonstall road off A646 west of the town centre, go through village and continue for 2 miles (3.2km). (See Point **5**.)

PARKING: 50

OPEN: all day; closed Monday lunchtime

FOOD: dinner only Tuesday to Friday; lunch & dinner Saturday; all day Sunday

BREWERY/COMPANY: free house

REAL ALE: Black Sheep Bitter, Thwaites, Moorhouses, guest beers

DOGS: allowed in garden only

Family facilities

There are no special facilities for children but there is a big box of toys in the games room that should keep youngsters amused on inclement days.

Alternative refreshment stops

Good range of pubs and cafés in Hebden Bridge, including the White Lion at Bridge Gate and the Fox & Goose on Heptonstall Road.

☛ Where to go from here

Head for Halifax and Eureka! The Museum for Children (www.eureka.org.uk). There are over 400 'must touch' exhibits and interactive activities in four main gallery spaces: Me and My Body, Living and Working Together, Our Global Garden and Invent, Create and Communicate. Children can find out how their bodies and senses work, discover the realities of daily life, travel from the familiar 'backyard' to amazing and far-away places and explore the world of communications.

Haworth's Brontë Moors

Across the wild Pennine moors to the romantic ruin of Top Withins.

The Brontës

Who could have imagined, when the Reverend Patrick Brontë became curate of the Church of St Michael and All Angels in 1820, that the little gritstone town of Haworth would become a literary hub to rival Grasmere and Stratford-upon-Avon? But it has, and visitors flock here in great numbers: some to gain some insights into the works of Charlotte, Emily and Anne, others just to enjoy a day out. The Georgian parsonage is a museum, restored to reflect the lives of the Brontës, its rooms filled with their personal treasures.

Tourism is no recent development; by the middle of the 19th century the first literary pilgrims were finding their way to Haworth. No matter how crowded this little town becomes (and those who value their

solitude should avoid visiting on a sunny summer weekend) it is always possible to escape to the moors that surround the town. You can follow, literally, in the footsteps of the three sisters as they sought freedom and inspiration, away from the stifling confines of the parsonage and the adjacent graveyard. As you explore these inhospitable moors, you'll get a greater insight into the literary world of the Brontës than those who stray no further than the souvenir shops and tea rooms of Haworth.

the walk

1 Take the cobbled lane up past the parsonage, signed to **Haworth Moor**. The lane soon becomes a paved field path that leads to the Haworth to Stanbury road. Walk left along the road and, after just 40yds (36m), take a left fork in **Cemetery Road**, signed to Penistone Hill. Continue along this quiet road to a T-junction.

Haworth

WEST YORKSHIRE

3h30 | **7.5 MILES** | **12 KM** | **LEVEL 123**

2 Take the track straight ahead, soon signed 'Brontë Way' and 'Top Withins', which curves onto the moors before descending to South Dean Beck where, a few paces before the Brontë Bridge, you'll find the Brontë Waterfall and Brontë Seat (a stone that resembles a chair). Cross the bridge and climb steeply uphill to a three-way sign.

3 Keep left, uphill, on a paved path signed 'Top Withins'. The path levels out to accompany a wall. Cross a beck; a gradual uphill climb brings you to a signpost by a ruined building. Take a short detour of 200yds (183m), left, uphill and now on the Pennine Way, to visit the ruin of Top Withins, in a location said to have inspired Wuthering Heights.

4 Return to the signpost, and continue downhill, signed to Stanbury and Haworth. You have a broad, easily followed track across the wide expanse of wild Pennine moorland.

5 Pass a white farmhouse – Upper Heights Cottage – then bear immediately left at a fork of tracks (signed as the Pennine Way). Walk past another building, Lower Heights Farm. After 500yds (456m) as the Pennine Way goes left, continue on the track straight ahead, to a lane head signed to Stanbury and Haworth. Follow the lane to meet a road near the village of Stanbury.

6 Bear right along the road through Stanbury, then take the first road on the

MAP: OS Explorer OL21 South Pennines

START/FINISH: Haworth; pay car park, near Brontë Parsonage; grid ref: SE 029373

PATHS: well-signed and easy to follow, 2 stiles

LANDSCAPE: open moorland

PUBLIC TOILETS: Central Park, Haworth

TOURIST INFORMATION: Haworth, tel 01535 642329

THE PUB: The Old White Lion, Haworth

🅛 A long walk with some climbing across open exposed moorland; for older, more experienced children

Getting to the start

Haworth is tucked away neatly above the Worth Valley in the folds of the bleak South Pennine moors, just 3 miles (4.8km) south west of Keighley off the A629 and A6033, and north west of Bradford.

Researched and written by:
Terry Marsh, John Morrison

Left: The Brontë Parsonage in Haworth
Right: Shop front in the popular town of Haworth

right, signed to Oxenhope, and cross the dam of **Lower Laithe Reservoir**. Immediately beyond the dam, bear left on a road that is soon reduced to a track uphill, to rejoin **Cemetery Road**.

7 From here you retrace your outward route: walk left along the road, soon taking a **gap stile** on the right, to follow the paved field path back into Haworth.

Haworth

WEST YORKSHIRE

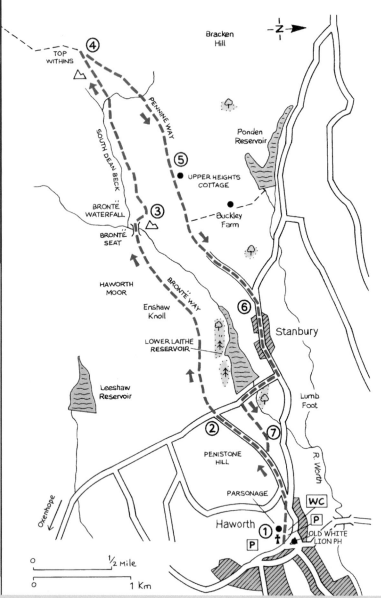

Bracken Hill

TOP WITHINS

PENNINE WAY

Ponden Reservoir

④

SOUTH DEAN BECK

⑤

UPPER HEIGHTS COTTAGE

BRONTË WATERFALL

③

Buckley Farm

BRONTË SEAT

BRONTË WAY

HAWORTH MOOR

Enshaw Knoll

⑥

Stanbury

LOWER LAITHE RESERVOIR

Lumb Foot

Leeshaw Reservoir

②

⑦

R. Worth

PENISTONE HILL

Oxenhope

PARSONAGE

WC

P

Haworth

①

P

OLD WHITE LION PH

0   ½ Mile

0   1 Km

The Old White Lion

A friendly, 300-year-old stone-built former coaching inn located at the top of a cobbled street in the heart of the town, and the place to stay if you are planning to visit the Brontë Parsonage Museum and explore the area. Gloriously beamed, oak-panelled and traditional furnished bars offer a welcome respite from the busy tourist trail. Here you can relax and enjoy pints of Theakston ales and tuck into some good honest bar food. Comfortable bedrooms, many with fine views over the town, offer up-to-date facilities.

Food
Jacket potatoes, giant filled Yorkshire puddings and sandwiches appear on the snack menu. From the carte, order braised lamb shank, home-made steak and kidney pudding, game casserole, Cajun chicken, or fillet steak of Old England.

Family facilities
Expect a warm welcome towards children. All ages are allowed inside, where there are high chairs and a children's menu.

Alternative refreshment stops
The Black Bull is Haworth's most famous public house, standing in the little cobbled square at the top of the steep main street. This is where Branwell Brontë came to drown his sorrows, and tried to forget the trauma of having such clever sisters. These days you can also have a sandwich, or a snack... or go for the Full Brontë.

☛ Where to go from here
Literary enthusiasts must visit the Brontë Parsonage Museum (www.bronte.org.uk). At the bottom of that famous cobbled

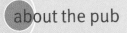

about the pub

The Old White Lion
West Lane, Haworth, Keighley
West Yorkshire BD22 8DU
Tel: 01535 642313
www.oldwhitelionhotel.com

DIRECTIONS:	town centre; 0.5 mile (800m) from Haworth Station
PARKING:	7
OPEN:	daily; all day
FOOD:	daily; all day Saturday & Sunday
BREWERY/COMPANY:	free house
REAL ALES:	Theakston Bitter & Black Bull, Tetley
DOGS:	not allowed inside
ROOMS:	14 en suite

street is Haworth Station on the restored Keighley and Worth Valley Railway (www.kwvr.co.uk). Take a steam train journey on Britain's last remaining complete branch line railway, or browse through the books and railway souvenirs at the station shop.

Oxenhope and the Worth Valley Railway

A moorland round and a return to the age of steam.

Oxenhope

Oxenhope is at the end of the line in more ways than one. As well as being the terminus of the Keighley and Worth Valley Railway, it is the last village in the Worth Valley. Oxenhope was a farming community that grew, like many other villages in West Yorkshire, with the textile industry. The mills have mostly gone, leaving the village to commuters who work in nearby towns.

The Keighley and Worth Valley line, running for 5 miles (8km) from Keighley to Oxenhope, is one of the longest established private railways in the country. It was built in 1867, funded by local mill owners, but the trains were run by the Midland Railway to link to the main Leeds–Skipton line at Keighley. When the line fell victim to Dr Beeching's axe in 1962, local rail enthusiasts banded together and the preservation society bought the line.

A regular timetable of trains has continued since 1968. Steam trains run every weekend throughout the year, and daily in summer. But the line doesn't just cater for tourists; locals in the Worth Valley appreciate the diesel services into Keighley that operate on almost 200 days per year.

The line runs through the heart of Brontë country, with stations at Oxenhope, Haworth, Oakworth, Danems, Ingrow and Keighley. The stations are a particular delight: fully restored, gas-lit and redolent of the age of steam. So when Edith Nesbitt's classic children's novel, *The Railway Children*, was filmed in 1970, the Keighley and Worth Valley Railway was a natural choice of setting.

the walk

1 From the entrance of Oxenhope Station take the minor road to the left, up to the A6033. Cross the road and take **Dark Lane** ahead, a sunken lane that goes steeply uphill. Follow this track to a road. Go right here, downhill, to join the **Denholme** road (B6141). Walk left along the road, up to the **Dog and Gun** pub, where you turn right on to Sawood Lane.

2 At **Coblin Farm**, your route becomes a rough track. Go through a gate to join a metalled road to the right, uphill, signed **Brontë Way**. After 100yds (91m), when the road accesses **Thornton Moor Reservoir**, walk straight ahead on an unmade track. Go through a gate into rough pasture, ignoring the Brontë Way sign to the right further on and staying on the main track.

MAP: OS Explorer OL21 South Pennines

START/FINISH: street parking in Oxenhope, near Keighley and Worth Valley Railway station; grid ref: SE 033354

PATHS: good paths and tracks, 6 stiles

LANDSCAPE: upland scenery, moor and pasture

PUBLIC TOILETS: none on route

TOURIST INFORMATION: Haworth, tel 01535 642329

THE PUB: Dog and Gun, Oxenhope

⚠ Almost half of this walk is on motorable roads without footpaths or verges, children will need to be closely supervised on these stretches

Getting to the start

Oxenhope lies in a remote valley 5 miles (8km) north west of Halifax and just a mile (1.6km) south of Haworth, and is best approached along the A6033, which runs northwards to Keighley and south to Hebden Bridge. The start is at the railway station, though parking here is for rail users only.

Researched and written by:
Terry Marsh, John Morrison

Oxenhope

WEST YORKSHIRE

3 At a fork, just 50yds (46m) further on, keep right as the track goes downhill towards a **transmission mast** on the mid-horizon. Pass a clump of trees, and cross a watercourse before descending to a minor road.

4 Go right here to pass a cattle grid and the mast. Just 150yds (138m) beyond the mast, as the road begins a steep descent, take a **wall stile** on the left. Go through another wall stile, to walk left, uphill, on a broad, walled track that deposits you at the **Waggon and Horses**.

5 Cross the road and take a track which bears right, steeply downhill. Where it bears sharp right again, after 300yds (274m), take a stile to the left, by a gate. Bear half-right and then follow a wall downhill to take three stiles in succession; at the bottom you meet a walled path. Go left here, cross a stream, and continue uphill to arrive at the entrance to **Lower Fold Farm**.

6 Follow the farm track to the right; turn right again, 20yds (18m) further on, at the end of a **cottage**, to join a metalled track. The track soon bears right above **Leeshaw Reservoir** and makes a gradual descent. Pass a mill to meet a road.

7 Cross the road and take the track ahead (signed to **Marsh**). Keep right of the first house, on a narrow walled path, then a paved path. Pass through the courtyard

what to look for

Visiting Oxenhope Station is like going back a hundred years. It has been lovingly restored, with enough period detail to make steam buffs dewy-eyed with nostalgia.

of a house as the path goes left, then right, and through a **kissing gate**. Follow a path between a wall and a fence to meet a walled lane. Go right here, passing **houses**, then on a field path to meet a road. Go right here and back down into **Oxenhope**.

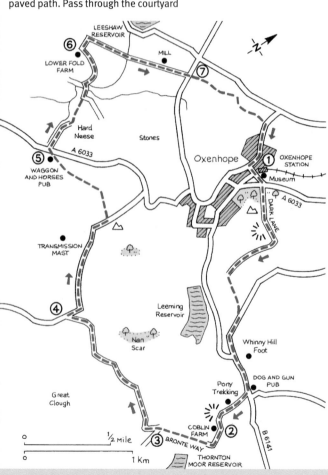

Dog and Gun

Set amid magnificent moorland in the heart of Brontë country above Oxenhope village, the final stop after Haworth on the Keighley and Worth Valley Railway, this stone-built 17th-century coaching inn is a welcoming refreshment stop during or after this invigorating walk. Reputedly haunted by the mischievous ghost of a former landlady who died after an accident in the pub, it is a popular, traditionally furnished local with roaring log fires in winter, a splendid pint of Timothy Taylor Landlord on tap, and a good range of home-cooked pub food to satisfy hearty walking appetites.

Food

The extensive menu offers a choice of sandwiches, filled jacket potatoes, fish and chips, Cumberland sausage, a chalkboard lists daily specials, and traditional roast lunches are always available on Sundays.

Family facilities

Although there are no special facilities for children they are welcome inside the pub and a children's menu is available.

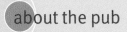

about the pub

Dog and Gun
Denholm Road, Oxenhope
West Yorkshire BD22 9SN
Tel: 01535 643159
www.dogandgun.com

DIRECTIONS: from Oxenhope take the B6141 towards Denholm; pub past Leeming Reservoir a mile (1.6km) east of the village, at point 2

PARKING: 30

OPEN: closed Monday

FOOD: no food Sunday evening

BREWERY/COMPANY: Timothy Taylor Brewery

REAL ALE: Timothy Taylor Landlord, guest beers

DOGS: not allowed inside

Alternative refreshment stops

Also on the route is the Waggon & Horses, an isolated pub on the Hebden Bridge Road out of Oxenhope. If you decide to take the train there's an excellent café at Oxenhope Station, appropriately enough in a stationary British Rail buffet car.

☞ Where to go from here

Take a trip to Haworth and back on the Keighley and Worth Valley Railway (www.kwvr.co.uk), and relive the great days of steam. While you're there explore the quaint cobbled streets and visit the Brontë Parsonage Museum (www.bronte.org.uk). You can return on foot along the Worth Way.

Along the Colne Valley

The rural valley between Slaithwaite and Marsden.

Colne Valley

Transport across the Pennine watershed has always faced problems. With the increase in trade between Yorkshire and Lancashire, another route across the Pennines was soon needed. The Huddersfield Narrow Canal links Huddersfield with Ashton-under-Lyne in Greater Manchester. Though only 20 miles (32.2km) long, it includes the Standedge Tunnel. Begun in 1798, and dug with pick, shovel and dynamite, the canal was opened to traffic in 1811.

The Colne Valley is lined with towns with evocative names – Milnsbridge, Linthwaite, Slaithwaite and Marsden – are threaded along the River Colne like beads

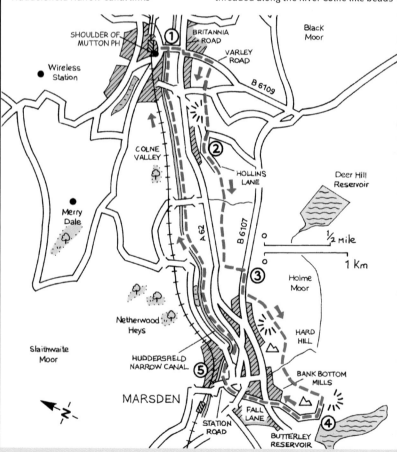

what to look for

When Enoch and James Taylor of Marsden started manufacturing cropping frames, they caused consternation amongst the shearers, who feared for their livelihoods. They realised that a single machine could do the work of many men. So, banded together as 'Luddites', the shearers attacked the mills where the hated frames were being introduced. The grave of Enoch Taylor can be seen on a small green you pass shortly after walking under the A62 and into Marsden.

3h00 — **7** MILES — **11.5** KM — **LEVEL** 123

MAP: OS Explorer OL21 South Pennines

START/FINISH: plenty of street parking in Slaithwaite; grid ref: SE 079140

PATHS: field paths, good tracks and canal tow path, 9 stiles

LANDSCAPE: typical South Pennine country, canalside

PUBLIC TOILETS: Slaithwaite and Marsden

TOURIST INFORMATION: Huddersfield, tel 01484 223200

THE PUB: Shoulder of Mutton, Slaithwaite

❶ The first half of the walk is tiring with steep ascents and descents

Getting to the start

Slaithwaite lies in the Colne Valley, and is best approached along the A62, either from Huddersfield or Oldham. The easiest place to park at the start is up near the railway station; there is usually room for on-street parking there.

Researched and written by:
Terry Marsh, John Morrison

...n a string. In the 18th century this was a landscape of scattered farms and hand-loom weavers, mostly situated on the higher ground, but the deep-cut valley of the Colne was transformed by the Industrial Revolution. Once the textile processes were mechanised, mills were built in the valley bottom by new industrial entrepreneurs.

Slaithwaite (often pronounced 'Slowitt') is typical of the textile towns in the Colne Valley: unpretentious and a little scruffy. It became an unlikely spa town, albeit briefly, when its mineral springs were compared favourably with those of Harrogate. A filled-in section of the canal at Slathwaite is being opened up, to bring water-borne traffic through the town.

the walk

1 Walk along **Britannia Road** up to the main A62 road. Cross over, turn right and take Varley Road up to the left. Beyond the last house go right, through a stile next to a **gate**. Join a grassy track across a field to a stile on the right-hand end of the wall ahead. Follow a wall to your right, across a stile, to a very minor road. Go right here, and follow the road left to a **T-junction**. Go straight ahead here, on a track; after just

The Marsden Canal next to the Tunnel End Canal and Countryside Museum

20yds (18m) bear left on a track between houses. Cross a stile by a gate on to a field path, with great views of the Colne Valley. Go forward to follow a **wall** on your right; towards its end go through a gap in the wall and take the steps, to continue in the same direction. After a **step stile**, keep to the right, slightly downhill, following a wall to another stile taking you on to a road.

2 Go right, along the road, for 20yds (18m), then left on to a metalled track (**Hollins Lane**). Continue as the track becomes rougher; when it peters out, keep left of an old **cottage** and go through a gate. Follow a field-edge path ahead, through a pair of gates either side of a beck. Pass a **ruined house** to descend on a walled path. When it bears sharp right keep straight ahead through a gate on to a field path. Follow a wall on your right; where it ends keep ahead, slightly uphill across two fields, and meet a walled track. Go left here, towards a **farm**. Go right, after 50yds (46m), over a stile on to another walled path downhill. The path soon bears right; take a stile to the left to follow a field-edge path. Cross another field and go left, uphill, where you meet a wall near an **unusual memorial**. Take a walled path up to the B6107.

3 Go right, along the road, for just 75yds (68m), and take a stony track to your left. Keep left of a house, via a **kissing gate**, as you get good views across Marsden and the head of the Colne Valley (there are a number

of paths that offer a more direct route down to Marsden, but you'll be missing out on the best views if you take a short-cut). About 150yds (138m) past the house bear right at a fork, taking the less obvious track. You soon follow a wall, beginning a slow descent. Across a **beck**, the track forks again; keep left, uphill, to skirt the shoulder of much-quarried **Hard Hill**. The track takes you steeply downhill, then up to a stile, then down again to cross a beck on a stone retaining wall. After another little climb, you have level walking and superb views, with **Butterley Reservoir** ahead of you. Bear left, steeply uphill, at a tiny **stone building**, cross two stiles and meet a tarmac track. Follow it right, downhill, to meet a road.

4 Go right, down the road, passing terraced houses dwarfed by **Bank Bottom Mills**. Keep straight ahead at the roundabout, down Fall Lane, soon bearing left to dip beneath the main road and into Marsden at **Towngate**. At the far end of a green, take Station Road, up to meet the **Huddersfield Narrow Canal**.

5 Opposite the Railway Inn, take a path on the right that soon goes down steps to join the canal tow path. Follow the canal for about 3 miles (4.8km) – passing beneath a road, past several locks and **pools**, between reservoirs, under two more road bridges – and eventually back into Slaithwaite.

A stretch of the Marsden Canal near Huddersfield

Shoulder of Mutton

Like the town in which it stands, the Shoulder of Mutton has no pretensions to grandeur, nor airs and graces. It's just a simple and friendly locals' pub at the end of the walk, serving simple, home-cooked pub food and first-class real ales from Northern breweries.

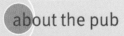

Food

A sandwich menu is only available at lunchtimes. Evening dishes include chicken curry, chilli, Cumberland sausage, ham and mushroom tagliatelle, seafood platter and a range of steaks and grills.

Family facilities

Children are welcome inside and a children's menu is available.

Alternative refreshment stops

You have a wide choice of pubs and cafés on this walk, in both Slaithwaite and Marsden. The Railway, close to the rail station and canal, in Marsden, comes at the halfway point.

☛ Where to go from here

Take a guided trip into the Standedge Tunnel (www.standedge.co.uk), the highest, longest and deepest canal tunnel in Britain and explore the Standedge Visitor Centre (children's play area).

about the pub

Shoulder of Mutton
9 Church Street, Slaithwaite
West Yorkshire HD7 5AS
Tel: 01484 844661

DIRECTIONS: see Getting to the start; the pub is on the corner of Church Street close to the railway station

PARKING: none (public car park nearby)

OPEN: daily; all day

FOOD: daily; all day; not evenings Saturday & Sunday

BREWERY/COMPANY: Punch Taverns

REAL ALE: Black Sheep Bitter, Timothy Taylor Landlord, Tetley, guest beers

DOGS: not allowed inside

Halifax and the Shibden Valley

WALK

An old packhorse track, a superb half-timbered hall and a hidden valley – all just a short walk from Halifax.

Halifax

Set amongst the Pennine hills, Halifax was a town in the vanguard of the Industrial Revolution. Its splendid civic buildings and huge mills are a good indication of the town's prosperity, won from the wool trade. Ironically, the most splendid building of all came close to being demolished. The Piece Hall, built in 1779, predates the industrial era. Here, in a total of 315 rooms on three colonnaded floors, the hand-weavers of the district would offer their wares (known as pieces) for sale to cloth merchants. The colonnades surround a massive square and your first reaction to the square may be surprise, for this is a building that recalls Renaissance Italy.

The mechanisation of the weaving process left the Piece Hall largely redundant. In the intervening years it has served a variety of purposes, including as a venue for political oration and as a wholesale market. During the 1970s, after narrowly escaping the wrecking ball, the Piece Hall was spruced up and now houses a museum, tourist information centre and small shops and businesses.

The cobbled thoroughfare that climbs so steeply up Beacon Hill is known as the Magna Via. Until 1741, when a turnpike road was built, this was the only practicable approach to Halifax from the east, for both foot and packhorse traffic. Also known as Wakefield Gate, the Magna Via linked up with the Long Causeway, the old high, level road to Burnley. The route was superseded in the 1820s by the turnpike through Godley Cutting. Today the Magna Via, too steep to be adopted for modern motor vehicles, remains a fascinating relic of the past.

Situated on a hill above Halifax, Shibden Hall is a magnificent half-timbered house set in 90 acres (36ha) of beautiful, rolling parkland. Dating from 1420, the hall has been owned by prominent local families – the Oates, Saviles, Waterhouses and, latterly, the Listers. All these families left their mark on the fabric of the house, but, the core of the original house remains intact. The rooms are furnished in period style, to show how they might have looked over almost six centuries.

The oak furniture and panelling has that patina of age that antique forgers try in vain to emulate. Barns and other buildings have been converted into a folk museum, with displays of old vehicles, tools and farm machinery. When Emily Brontë created Thrushcross Grange in *Wuthering Heights*, she may have had Shibden Hall in mind. It certainly proved a suitable location in 1991 for a new film version of the famous story.

the walk

1 From the car park go uphill along the main drive; just before you meet the main A58 road, bear right across grass and down **Old Godley Lane**. Pass houses and take steps up to the main road at the busy junction of **Stump Cross**.

2 Cross over the road with care at traffic lights, and go left past the **Stumps Cross Inn** and take **Staups Lane** on the right. Walk up the lane, which soon

2h30 — 4.5 MILES — 7.2 KM — LEVEL 123

...ecomes cobbled, to meet another ...urfaced road. Bear left here, down a ...etalled track, through a gate, to join a ...traight, double-paved track into **Shibden** **Dale**. When the paving ends, continue via ... gate and through open pasture. Turn left, ...t the next gate, walking down a lane that ...oon leads you to **The Shibden Mill Inn**.

3 Walk past the inn to the far end of the car park, to join a track that crosses **Shibden Beck**. Continue right at a fork, ...nd beyond a brick-built house, the track ...arrows to a walled path. You emerge from ...ountryside, to walk past the houses of **Claremont** and then bear right to cross ...he main A58 road, as it goes through the ...teep-sided **Godley Cutting**, on a bridge. ...ake a set of steps immediately after the ...ridge and walk left along the road.

...hibden Hall dates from the 15th century

MAP: OS Explorer 288 Bradford & Huddersfield

START/FINISH: parking in Shibden Park; grid ref: SE 095254

PATHS: old packhorse tracks and field paths

LANDSCAPE: surprisingly rural, considering the proximity to Halifax

PUBLIC TOILETS: at start

TOURIST INFORMATION: Halifax, tel 01422 368725

THE PUB: The Shibden Mill Inn, Shibden Mill

Getting to the start

Shibden Park is on the eastern outskirts of Halifax, just off the A58 at Stumps Cross. The start is just one mile from the city centre.

Researched and written by: Terry Marsh, John Morrison

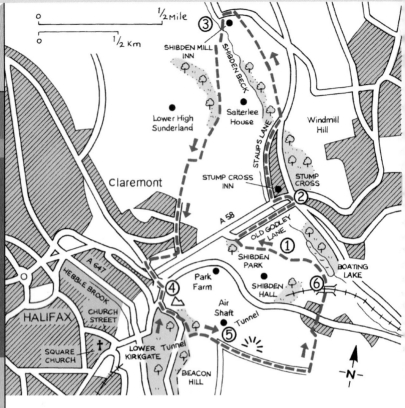

4 At a road junction (signed for Southowram) bear left. Just after the entrance to a **warehous**e (Aquaspersion), take a cobbled path on the left that makes a steep ascent up **Beacon Hill**.

5 This old packhorse track – known as the **Magna Via** – joins another path and continues uphill to a large retaining wall, where you have a choice of tracks. Keep left on a **cinder track**, slightly downhill, as views open up of the surprisingly rural Shibden Valley. Keep left when the track forks again; after a further 100yds (91m) take a walled path on the left (signed to **Stump Cross**). Follow a hedgerow downhill through a little estate of new houses to a road. Cross here and take a gated path immediately to the right of a **farm entrance**,

which takes you downhill, under the railway line and into **Shibden Park**, close to the boating lake.

6 Bear left along the **lake** edge, and then follow the main drive to return to the start.

what to look for

The birds-eye view of Halifax from Beacon Hill is well worth the effort of climbing it. A century ago this view would have looked very different: most people's idea of William Blake's 'dark satanic mills' were here in unhealthy profusion, casting a dense pall of sulphurous smoke over the valley.

The Shibden Mill Inn

This picturesque whitewashed inn is tucked away in a leafy hollow of the Shibden Valley with a stream rushing noisily nearby. The 17th-century inn has been sympathetically renovated to retain its original charm, with low beams, antique furniture, big log fires, rugs on floors, cushioned benches, rustic tables with candles, and hunting prints on the walls. It's a really cosy place in which to relax, and there's a wide choice of real ales and wines to accompany some seriously good pub food. When the weather is kind, the attractive, heated, riverside terrace is the place to be. There are super, individually decorated en suite bedrooms for those finding it difficult to leave.

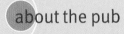

about the pub

The Shibden Mill Inn
Shibden Mill, Shibden
Halifax, West Yorkshire HX3 7UL
Tel: 01422 365840
www.shibdenmillinn.com

DIRECTIONS: signposted off the A58, 1 mile east of Halifax (see Point **3**)	
PARKING: 100	
OPEN: daily; all day	
FOOD: daily; all day Sunday	
BREWERY/COMPANY: free house	
REAL ALE: Theakston XB, John Smiths, Moorhouses Bitter, guest beers	
DOGS: allowed in the pub	
ROOMS: 14 en suite	

Food
Bar meals take in imaginative sandwiches with home-made bread, ham, egg and chips and macaroni cheese. On the carte you may find pork shank with chorizo, cabbage and potato, sea bass with crab tart and roasted artichokes, and iced white chocolate parfait.

Family facilities
Families will love this place; there's a genuine welcome to children, with high chairs, a decent menu and smaller portions available, and colouring materials and board games to keep youngsters amused.

Alternative refreshment stops
The Stump Cross Inn at Shibden.

☛ Where to go from here
You should take the children to Eureka! The Museum for Children (www.eureka.org.uk), the ultimate in hands-on discovery museums. It is designed specifically for children up to the age of 12, with over 400 interactive exhibits exploring science, nature and the world around you. There's also Piece Hall, which houses an art gallery and several craft shops, and Shibden Hall, an early 15th-century house where rooms have been laid out to illustrate life in different periods of its history.

Shipley Glen's Tramway and Baildon Moor

WALK

A glimpse of moorland and a traditional rural playground for the mill workers of Shipley and Saltaire.

Shipley Glen

For the people of Shipley and Saltaire, Baildon Moor has traditionally represented a taste of the countryside on their doorsteps. Mill-hands could leave the mills and cramped terraced streets behind, and breathe clean Pennine air. They could listen to the song of the skylark and the bubbling cry of the curlew. There were heather moors to tramp across, gritstone rocks to scramble up and, at Shipley Glen, springy sheep-grazed turf on which to spread out a picnic blanket. There was also a funfair to visit –

not a little funfair, like there still is today – but a veritable theme park.

Towards the end of the 19th century, Shipley Glen was owned by a Colonel Maude who created a number of attractions. Visitors could enjoy the sundry delights of the Switchback Railway, Marsden's Menagerie, the Horse Tramway and the Aerial Runway. More sedate pleasures could be found at the Camera Obscura, the boating lake in the Japanese garden, and the Temperance Tea Room and Coffee House. Sam Wilson, a local entrepreneur, played his own part in developing Shipley Glen. In 1895 he created the Shipley Glen Tramway. Saltaire people could now stroll through Roberts Park, past the steely-gazed statue of Sir Titus Salt, and enjoy the tram-ride to the top of the glen. Thousands of people would

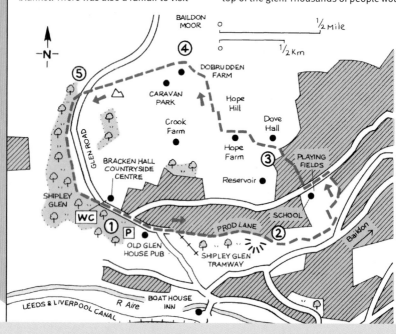

clamber, each weekend, on to the little cable-hauled 'toast-rack' cars. As one car went up the hill, another car would descend on an adjacent track.

In commercial terms, the heyday of Shipley Glen was during the Edwardian era. On busy days as many as 17,000 people would take the tramway up to the pleasure gardens. Losing out to more sophisticated entertainments, however, Shipley Glen went into a slow decline. Most of the attractions are now gone, but not all. You can still ride the Aerial Runway (though it's not exactly a white-knuckle ride) and spend some money at the little funfair. Best of all, you can still take the tramway, which runs every day from May to September, with more restrictive operation during the winter. The Old Glen House is still a popular pub, though the Temperance Tea Room and Coffee House have been transformed into the Bracken Hall Countryside Centre. Local people still enjoy the freedom of the heather moorland. Despite all the changes, Shipley Glen retains a stubbornly old-fashioned air, and is all the better for it.

the walk

1 Walk down Glen Road, passing the **Old Glen House** pub. Continue as the road becomes Prod Lane, signed as a cul-de-sac. Pass the tiny funfair and the entrance to the **Shipley Glen Tramway**. Where the road ends, keep straight ahead to locate an enclosed path to the right of a house. Follow this path, with houses on your left, and woodland to your right. As you come to a **metal barrier**, ignore a path to the left. Keep straight on downhill. 100yds (91m) beyond the barrier, you have a choice of

2h30 — **4 MILES** — **6.4 KM** — **LEVEL 1** 2 3

MAP: OS Explorer 288 Bradford & Huddersfield

START/FINISH: Shipley: on Glen Road, between Bracken Hall Countryside Centre and Old Glen House pub; grid ref: SE 132389

PATHS: moor and field paths

LANDSCAPE: moorland, fields and gritstone rocks

PUBLIC TOILETS: at Bracken Hall Countryside Centre; also near Old Glen House pub and in Saltaire

TOURIST INFORMATION: Bradford, tel 01274 433678

THE PUB: Old Glen House, Baildon

Getting to the start

Finding the moorland road above Shipley Glen requires a certain amount of accurate map reading. It lies about 2 miles (1km) north west of Shipley, and is best reached through the residential area of Baildon (off the A6038), from where a good road runs through the edge of a housing estate out onto the moors.

Researched and written by:
Terry Marsh, John Morrison

paths; bear left here, uphill, soon getting good views over Saltaire, Shipley and the Aire Valley.

2 Beyond the woodland, continue to walk beneath a quarried sandstone cliff. When you come to an open area, with panoramic views, take a set of **stone steps**, with metal handrails, up to the top of the cliff. Bear right on a path between chain-link fences, which takes you around **school playing fields**, to meet a road. Walk left along the road for 150yds (138m). When you are level with the school on your left, cross the road and take a narrow, enclosed path on the right, between houses. Walk gradually uphill, crossing a road in a **housing estate** and picking up the enclosed path again. Soon, at a kissing gate, you emerge into pasture.

3 Go half left, uphill, to a kissing gate at the top-left corner of the field. Before you reach the farm you see ahead, join the access track, walking past the **buildings** on a cinder track till a metal gate bars your way. Go right here, through a wooden gate, on a path between walls. Beyond the next gate you come out on to **Baildon Moor**. Your path is clear, following a wall to your left. Keep straight on, as the wall curves to the left, towards the next farm (and caravan

Previous page: Heather at Shipley Glen
Above: Walking in the trees above Shipley Glen

park). Cross a metalled farm track and curve left to follow the boundary wall of **Dobrudden Farm**.

4 Walk gradually downhill towards **Bingley** in the valley. When the wall bears left, keep straight ahead, through bracken, more steeply downhill. Cross a metalled track and carry on down to meet **Glen Road** again.

5 Follow the path along the rocky edge of wooded Shipley Glen leading you back to the **Bracken Hall Countryside Centre** and your car.

what to look for

Call in at the Bracken Hall Countryside Centre on Glen Road, which has a number of interesting displays about the history of Shipley Glen, its flora and its fauna. There are also temporary exhibitions on particular themes, interactive features and a programme of children's activities throughout the year. The gift shop sells maps, guides, natural history books and ice creams.

Old Glen House

High above Saltaire and close to the Shipley Glen Tramway, the Old Glen House was built to serve the Saltaire folk escaping the mills for some rest and relaxation in Shipley's pleasure gardens during Edwardian times. It remains popular and is a delightful old pub with oak beams, stone walls and warming open fires. The welcoming bars are decorated with a wealth of sporting memorabilia and you'll also find a good locals' bar with wide-screen TV, and a games room. On warmer days you can make good use of the terrace and beer garden.

Food

Bar food includes a good range of simple snacks and sandwiches as well as main courses such as beef chilli, Mediterranean chicken, and Sunday roast beef and Yorkshire pudding lunches.

Family facilities

Expect a warm welcome towards children; they are welcome throughout the pub and there's a children's menu and a play area in the beer garden.

Alternative refreshment stops

If heading off to visit Saltaire, you could try the Boat House Inn. Situated next to the River Aire, it was Sir Titus Salt's private boathouse, built in 1871. You can enjoy your meal or drink on a little terrace overlooking the river.

☛ Where to go from here

Make sure you visit Salts Mill in Saltaire (www.saltsmill.org.uk), a giant of a building on a truly epic scale. At the height of production 3,000 people worked here. There were 1,200 looms clattering away, weaving as much as 30,000 yards of cloth every working day. The mill is a little quieter these days – with a permanent exhibition of artworks by David Hockney, another of Bradford's most famous sons. In Bradford, you can visit Europe's only Museum of Colour (www.sdc.org.uk), which is packed with visitor-operated exhibits demonstrating the effects of light and colour. At the National Museum of Photography, Film and Television (www.nmpft.org.uk) you can experience the past, present and future of photography, film and television, with ten amazing galleries and a spectacular 3D IMAX cinema.

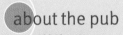

about the pub

Old Glen House
Prod Lane, Baildon
Shipley, West Yorkshire BD17 5BN
Tel: 01274 589325

DIRECTIONS:	see Getting to the start
PARKING:	50
OPEN:	daily; all day
FOOD:	daily; no food Monday to Wednesday evening
BREWERY/COMPANY:	Punch Taverns
REAL ALE:	Timothy Taylor Landlord & Best, Tetley
DOGS:	allowed inside

Shipley Glen

WEST YORKSHIRE

A circuit around Holmfirth

Follow in the footsteps of TV's Last of the Summer Wine characters on their South Pennine adventures.

Summer Wine Country

Holmfirth and the Holme Valley have been popularised as 'Summer Wine Country'. The whimsical TV series, starring the trio of incorrigible old buffers Compo, Foggy and Clegg, which ran for over a quarter of a century.

Holmfirth town, much more than just a film set, is the real star – along with the South Pennine scenery that surrounds it. By the time you have completed half of this walk, you are a mile (1.6km) from the Peak National Park. The town grew rapidly with the textile trades, creating a tight-knit community in the valley bottom: a maze of ginnels, alleyways and narrow lanes. The River Holme, which runs through its middle, has flooded on many occasions. But the most devastating flood occurred in 1852 when, after heavy rain, Bilberry Reservoir burst its banks. The resulting torrent of water destroyed the centre of Holmfirth and claimed 81 lives. The tragedy was reported at length on the front page of the *London Illustrated News*. A public subscription fund was started to help the flood survivors rebuild the town. These traumatic events are marked by a monument near the bus station.

the walk

1 From Crown Bottom car park, walk to the right along **Huddersfield Road** for just 100yds (91m) before bearing left opposite the fire station, up **Wood Lane**. The road soon narrows to a steep track. Keep left of a house and through a gate,

to continue on a walled path. At the top of the hill, by a bench, follow the track to the right. Follow this track, soon enclosed, as it wheels left, down into a valley. Soon after you approach **woodland**, you have a choice of tracks: keep left on the walled path, uphill. Join a more substantial **farm track** and, 100yds (91m) before the cottage ahead, look for a wall stile on the left. Follow a field path to emerge, between houses, in **Upperthong**. Turn right into the village, past a pub to a T-junction.

2 Bear left along the road, which wheels round to the right. Walk downhill, with great views opening up of the Holme Valley. After 150yds (138m) on the road, take a cinder track on the right. Walk down past **Newlands Farm** to meet a road. Cross over and take the lane ahead, steeply down into a little valley and up the other side. When this minor road forks at the top, go right, uphill. Immediately after the first house, go left, on a gravel track (**Hogley Lane**). Follow this track to **Lower Hogley Farm** where you keep right, past a knot of houses, to a gate/stile and on to a field path, with a wall to your left. Over a stile, cross the next field, now with the wall to your right. Past the next wall stile, veer half left across the next field (aim for the **mast** on the horizon). After one more field, descend to a road.

3 Go right for just 50yds (46m) to bear left around an **old schoolhouse** on a grassy path. Follow the walled path downhill, through a gate; as the path opens out into a grassy area, bear left on a grassy track

The river Holme running through Holmfirth, scene of a much-loved TV series

| 3h00 | 4.5 MILES | 7.2 KM | LEVEL 2 |

WALK

MAP: OS Explorer 288 Bradford & Huddersfield
START/FINISH: centre of Holmfirth gets very crowded, so park in Crown Bottom car park (pay-and-display) on Huddersfield Road; grid ref: SE 143084
PATHS: good paths and tracks, 8 stiles
LANDSCAPE: upland pasture
PUBLIC TOILETS: Holmfirth
TOURIST INFORMATION: Holmfirth, tel 01484 222444
THE PUB: Old Bridge Hotel, Holmfirth
🛈 Although the walk is not long, there is a long (and initially steep) ascent, and a long descent, which could be tiring for very young children

Getting to the start
Holmfirth lies tucked away in the Holme Valley on the A6024 6 miles (9.7km) south of Huddersfield, from where it is easily reached. Pay-and-display parking on Huddersfield Road.

Researched and written by:
Terry Marsh, John Morrison

Holmfirth

WEST YORKSHIRE

down into the valley. Follow a high wall on your right, over a stile, on to an enclosed path. On approaching **houses**, take a stile and join a metalled track at a fork. Bear right here, then immediately left, on a narrow path between houses. Follow a field path through a gate; pass houses and a **mill** down to meet the main A6024 road.

4 Cross the road; by a row of diminutive **cottages** take Old Road to the left. Keep straight ahead at a junction down **Water Street**. Beyond a mill, cross the River Holme on a metal footbridge and follow a riverside path. Soon the path veers right through pasture; when the path forks, keep right, uphill, to enter woodland. Continue in the same direction, uphill, passing an old quarry. When the path forks near a post, bear right, uphill once more, to emerge

what to look for

Holmfirth seems to have grown up without much help from town planners. It is an intriguing maze of ginnels, stone steps and small cobbled alleyways, rising up between little gritstone houses. After a few minutes climb you will be rewarded with a splendid view over the roofscape of the town.

from the wood on to a **field path**. Cross two fields to join a track by a house. Pass more **cottages** to meet a road.

5 Go left, along the road. You should enjoy splendid views down into the **Holme Valley**, as you make the long descent back to Holmfirth.

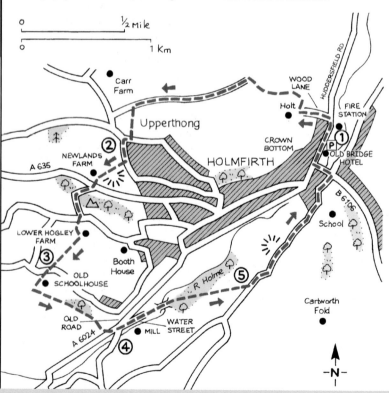

Old Bridge Hotel

At the heart of Holmfirth and 'Summer Wine' country, the Old Bridge is a comfortable hotel with spacious, modernised bar rooms sporting beams and paintings of Yorkshire scenes. Surprisingly, for a hotel, it serves an impressive range of real ales, and food is served all day. Members of the cast from the famous TV series were a common sight in the bar, as they regularly stayed here during filming.

Food
The wide-ranging menu lists sandwiches, hot filled baguettes, pasta and broccoli bake, lasagne, steak and kidney pie, cod wrapped in bacon, and braised lamb shank.

Family facilities
Families are welcome in the hotel and there's a good value children's menu.

Alternative refreshment stops
With so many visitors, Holmfirth is well supplied with pubs and tea shops. Compo's Café, smack in the centre of town, will already be familiar to fans of *Last of the Summer Wine*.

☞ Where to go from here
If you continue to drive through Holmfirth on the A6024, you pass Holmbridge, then Holme, before the Holme Valley comes to a dramatic end, surrounded by a huge sweep of rugged moorland. As you climb steeply to the height of Holme Moss, topped with a TV mast, you enter the Peak National Park.

about the pub

Old Bridge Hotel
Market Walk, Holmfirth
West Yorkshire HD7 1DA
Tel: 01484 681212
www.oldbridgehotel.com

DIRECTIONS: town centre, just south of the car park and start point of the walk	
PARKING: 30	
OPEN: daily; all day	
FOOD: daily; all day Sunday	
BREWERY/COMPANY: free house	
REAL ALE: Timothy Taylor Landlord, Black Sheep Bitter, guest beers	
DOGS: not allowed inside	
ROOMS: 20 en suite	

Acknowledgements

The Automobile Association would like to thank the following photo library for their assistance in the preparation of this book.

Photolibrary.com front cover b.

The following photographs are held in the Automobile Association's own photo library (AA World Travel Library) and were taken by the following photographers:

Jeff Beazley 4, 113, 114; Malc Birkitt 132; E A Bowness 12; Steve Day 108/9, 110; Derek Forss 76, 77; Anthony J Hopkins 144, 172, 173; Caroline Jones 140/1; Tom Mackie 15; Terry Marsh front cover cl, ccl, ccr, cr, 17, 19, 20/1, 22, 23, 24/5, 25b, 27, 28, 29, 31, 32/3, 35, 37, 39, 40/1, 41t, 43, 45, 46, 47, 48, 49, 51, 52, 53, 55, 56/7, 59, 61t, 61b, 63, 64, 64/5, 67, 69, 71, 72, 73, 75, 79, 80, 82, 83, 84, 85, 87, 88, 89, 91, 92, 93, 95, 96, 97, 99, 100/1, 101, 103, 106 107, 111, 115, 119, 120/1, 122, 123, 125t, 125b, 127, 128/9, 129, 131, 135, 136/7 138, 139, 143, 147, 151, 155, 159, 163, 167, 170, 171, 175; S & O Matthews 105; John Morrison 8/9; John Mottershaw 156/7, 161; Tony Souter 14b; Martin Trelawny 162; Wyn Voysey 13, 14t; Jonathan Welsh 116, 116/7; Peter Wilson 165; Linda Whitwam 9, 149t, 149b, 152, 153.